Dear M
Best ...
on your jo...
Your friend,
[signature]

The Unexplored Room

The Unexplored Room

❦

Dare to enter and find your heart

Greg Loewen

How to Contact the Author:

You can reach Dr. Greg Loewen by visiting this book's website: www.gregloewen.com.

ISBN: 0692751858
ISBN-13: 9780692751855

Contents

Acknowledgments

I am grateful to the mentors, sponsors, and coaches who challenged me and helped me find the connection between my heart and my power; to therapists and facilitators whose symbolic spaces became a drama school for my own drama; and to elders and guides who helped me to consider what to do with the time I have left on this planet. I am grateful for Samir Selmanovic PhD, who has given so much of himself in our hours of conversation and to Gregory V. Loewen, PhD, for his friendship, insight, and inspiration.

I am also grateful for my friends and family, who have read patiently, listened to me repeatedly, and encouraged me onward. And I am especially grateful for the inspiration from my children—Kris, Jen, and Katie—who have found a spiritual path I did not discover until I was much older. But greater than all this is the gratitude I have for my life partner, Suzi. Our unexplored rooms first connected forty years ago. This book would not exist without her.

Introduction

In many ways, this is a book about the forbidden and the unacceptable. It is about the things our parents didn't want to talk about. It is also about the things our culture deemed inappropriate when we were growing up. Perhaps you are wondering why someone gave you this book or why you were drawn to even pick it up. Why would *anyone* want to read about this kind of stuff?

Why indeed.

Despite our best efforts, our own unseen material lingers on silently, like a living entity in the basement. We might not remember putting it there, but when it surfaces, it can be quite disruptive. This forbidden, unacceptable stuff may be interfering with our lives already, if we look carefully.

We can spot elements of what we don't want to look at in ourselves, if we take a moment to notice the very things we hate about other people. We might notice the memories that we have been avoiding when something triggers childhood pain or trauma in our adult lives, or we might discover it within those things we believe we could never become. This is exactly where this material likes to hide.

Silently and invisibly, these are the very things that hijack us to destinations we weren't planning to visit. The things we were taught to avoid doing and talking about as we grew up are all stored away in a place I like to call "the unexplored room."

If we ever work in this space and gain access to the discarded aspects of ourselves, we become more whole. Our living space doubles. Being *whole* is a lot more complicated than being *happy*. While this book does not exactly claim to bring happiness, it does describe a kind of wholeness that happens when we are able to claim and own the things that we have been avoiding. This ownership of our interior is what gives us the strength to show up for what is difficult. Being whole enables us to face what is.

The fact is, as life unfolds, we eventually realize we are all haunted by those things our parents didn't want to talk about and by what our society and culture taught us to be unacceptable. Eventually we figure out that we want to recover from something.

Addiction is a metaphor for the human condition. It isn't just about alcohol or drugs. It isn't just sex or relationships. It isn't just about power, money, religion, or workaholism. Sometimes we want to recover from a serious illness and everything that surrounds being sick. Addiction is an illness, but any illness can be like an addiction, too.

In our lives, we eventually all want recovery from something or another. Recovery in those of us with alcoholism or drug addiction exposes a common thread that runs through the fabric of everyone's experience. And if we ever decide to try to recover from something, we are forced to face the hidden and suppressed material that lives on within our own interior.

Life *is* recovery. It is about playing the wrong note, then recovering. If you listen to certain jazz solos, you will hear what sounds like a mistake, but then the musical line shifts. You will hear recovery, as the "mistake" turns into art and beauty. Jazz legend Miles Davis once observed, "There are no mistakes." As a musician, he knew a good solo is less about technique and more about spontaneity and authenticity. Jazz is about noticing the unexpected, then playing with it.

In a similar way, every stand-up comic has told a joke that bombs, but those who are the funniest know how to recover from a failed joke. They don't blame the audience. They point out that their joke just bombed and make a joke about it. Comedy is recovery from the bomb. Every long-term relationship bombs sometimes, too. Relationships aren't just about natural chemistry (which is good) or commitment (which can be good, too); they're about betrayal, disappointment, and then recovery. Recovery contains the beauty, depth, and meaning we all hunger for in life.

Who am I to write such a book? I'm a physician who has struggled with addiction, among other things. I have been in recovery for more than twenty years. When I was desperate to learn how to stay clean and sober, I had to enter my own unexplored room. My own darkish secrets and hidden wounds were the source of a pain that fueled my search for pain relievers. Am I unique? No. I'm unique only because I talk openly about where our ordinary struggles come from.

Greg Loewen

Because of my determination to stay in recovery from addiction, I was forced to do a kind of personal work with my own material, and this has sustained my very life for many years. For some of us, this kind of work is the only way we can stay on the planet. What follows are the stories about what happens when someone dares to enter his or her hidden interior. They are stories of how I unwrapped my own shadow and found my heart.

What is so extraordinary about this work? The results. The impact of a reunion with the lost parts of our selves brings an extraordinary transformation. Everyone is permanently changed when they enter this place.

No matter what we struggle with, each of us finds some way of medicating our hidden pain, even if we don't want to talk about it. I have taken care of sick patients for more than thirty years, and I am grateful to have listened as they explored what their illnesses seem to be saying to them. Many experience the fear that comes from a serious illness and ask why it is happening in the first place. It requires uncommon courage to talk about our pain, especially if it originates from deep issues that are hurtful or forbidden within our hearts. I treasure such conversations. The root of the word *courage* is *coeur*, which means "heart." If our dialogue requires courage, then it has become wholehearted—*any* dialogue about our hidden pain is wholehearted.

Have you ever mused, perhaps during an election season, that a little therapy wouldn't kill one politician or another? An inescapable truth becomes clearer as we grow older: we all have stuff to work on. And I think most modern therapists would agree that our "stuff" is found within a place that has been called "the human shadow." This is the unconscious part of the human interior we all share. The book you're holding is a first-person expedition into this territory. This is a trip that challenges the notion that the shadow is our darker side or is some kind of "demon" we should fear; instead, it shows how the human shadow is a neutral space hidden beneath the figurative house where each of us lives. And it is a good and safe place for us to visit and to work.

You may decide to read this book in a whirlwind of a few days if you are hungry for its message—perhaps you can't get it in fast enough. But you may experience some intense emotions as you go through it; if so, please be gentle with yourself. Some decide to read it more slowly, even as a morning devotional over a period of weeks. Either way, I hope my journey will leave you with a new kind of map for your own inner landscape.

This book is a guided tour of the strangely familiar, and it comes with a simple word picture of our interior. This image of the unexplored room can help you to orient when you return to your life; the moment this happens, it will click all of a sudden. You will recognize where you are standing. You have seen this before. You will know you are experiencing something that has surfaced from your own unexplored room.

I had a similar experience when I started this work many years ago. It was when I first saw how my adoption-related wounds from childhood were getting in my way as an adult. At that moment, I changed forever. You will experience similar moments of clarity, too, if you decide to try this work for yourself.

Greg Loewen

This is the recovery we all want in life. If we want to be free from our pain relievers, then we have to look at the source of our pain. We have to acknowledge the wound. I will share how I greeted and healed the wounds from my past. But don't get me wrong: This is not a typical self-help book. I am not trying to tell you what to do. Instead, I am just sharing stories about what it was like for me to experience personal work, mostly within the territory of secular spirituality. At the end of each chapter, I include a short reflection, so you can sit with what you have just read. These brief meditations can provide you with a sense of what it is like to work with me in person.

Although this book might have an autobiographical quality, it is not intended to be my memoir, as colorful as that might seem. Instead, it is my intention to share what you might not typically hear from your doctor, with examples from gritty reality. These are stories I share with patients or clients when it seems my experiences would help them. Over the years, many have shared their personal stories with me, too, and these were the exchanges that changed my life for the better. Good ideas are a lot more powerful when they are personal, and the unexplored room is personal.

Personal work is something anyone can do, but sometimes our reluctance to ask for help is tied to a sense of shame. It is not rare for some religious traditions to make personal work more difficult by shaming those who struggle with life issues, such as addiction or broken marriages—this was the case for me. Religion might say to us, "If only you were more spiritual, then you wouldn't have these problems."

But religion isn't the only voice with this kind of message: We live in a society that tends to disparage personal work. If a politician is accused of seeking treatment for mental illness, then his or her campaign is probably over. Even if we use a softer, gentler term for mental illness (such as *stress* or *unwellness*), some still view getting help as a form of weakness. I have found that the opposite is true in my own life. Doing personal work is at the core of good leadership.

I hate to admit it, but there is another shame-based mechanism that underlies why men don't want to ask for help: the male ego. When in the driver's seat, we typically don't like to ask for directions. We're even less likely to ask for help when some kind of personal or psychological crisis arises. There is a stigma around anyone who dares to ask for help, but I hope my openness about doing personal work will show how ordinary and natural it is to acknowledge our humanity.

Many of us sense that we have issues but hesitate to look inward because of fear. We might have painful secrets from our past that we have decided to forget, such as trauma in adulthood or abuse from childhood. We may no longer possess any memory of the trauma or abuse if we unconsciously stifled it long ago. But regardless of what memories we may have access to, deep fear may rise to the surface when we consider looking inward, and we may find ourselves asking, "How could I ever face that awful stuff?"

One of my intentions as I wrote these words was to try to dissolve the fear of acknowledging the material found in our unexplored rooms. It is possible to do this work and maintain our personal safety. We can open the door gently, as we ask ourselves if we are ready to explore. No matter what we may find there, someone somewhere has already faced it—we are not alone. A few of my own stories could create sensational headlines, but if you read onward with an open heart, you will find the real headline reads, "You Can Work on Your Stuff." I did.

None of us can see our own unexplored rooms very well, but the stuff in these rooms is often visible to others. Sometimes, the work we need the most is more obvious to those around us than it is to ourselves. When we eventually decide to work on our stuff, those who know us the best are likely to say something like, "Finally!" or "Thank God!" Sometimes we are the last to see the obvious.

If you have felt stuck with some recurrent addiction (anything from alcohol and drugs to food and shopping), you will read about how I healed the pain we all try to medicate away. If you have silently lived with depression or have ever contemplated suicide, I have been there, too, and I wrote this book especially for you (please see the Safety Warning in the Appendix).

If you have struggled with failed relationships, you might recognize something old and familiar that has gotten between you and your partner. If you have parented your child and found yourself making the same mistakes you hated when *you* were a child, I will describe how I worked to rewrite this part of my own story.

If you have become disillusioned in your work space, you may read my story and catch yourself looking inward to see something you used to love about your work.

If a serious illness has pushed you to look at your own mortality, or if you care for someone at the end of his or her life, you may identify with my own struggle around death-related issues that surfaced when I faced serious illness.

What would our society be like if we really thought working on our stuff was OK? What if we believed personal work was really a form of internal fitness training? Our divorce rate would decline, for one. Our problems with addiction, alcoholism, obesity, and debt would shrink. How would our politicians behave if they had worked on their stuff? I bet there might be fewer wars and embarrassing sex scandals. How would we treat one another in business, education, law enforcement, and health care if we all had worked on our stuff?

In our journey through the unexplored room, I assume that every-one has issues and that we all have been made in the same way. In the pages that follow, you will find a trustworthy, well-respected doctor and scientist who has worked on his stuff. Many of us out here in the real world have worked on our stuff. If someone ever treats you with unusual empathy and understanding during a crisis, then you probably just met one of us.

My background as a clinical scientist with research and teaching experience led me to honor the domain of science, but in this book, I have been chiefly informed by my own transformation. These are personal experiences that I am ready to share. I am at a point in my life where my heart is full. I have found incredible healing and am now living in a space I never could have imagined when I was younger—and it is only because of doing this work. Healing and transformation: these are the results of work anyone can do. Welcome to the unexplored room.

Chapter One
The Unexplored Room

A stick, a stone
It's the end of the road,
It's a little alone.
It's a sliver of glass,
It is life,
It's the sun.
It is night,
It is death.
It's a trap,
It's a gun.

—Antonio Carlos Jobim

"The Waters of March" has always fascinated me. I have heard this song in my dreams. With cryptic lyrics, Jobim draws a menagerie of objects, animals, and events that drift past the banks of a flooded river in the springtime. When the water is high enough, everything washes downstream. Everything unseen eventually floats to the surface in Jobim's river.

Greg Loewen

The unexplored room is a little like this: There are treasures, dangers, and long-forgotten things down there. And when the floodwater rises, we have little control over what is exposed.

Imagine for a moment that you have spent your life inside the old house of your childhood. You know every detail of your family home. In your mind, you can easily picture the living room, the subtleties of the dining room, the bathroom fixtures, the kitchen layout, and all the bedrooms. One day, you decide to clean out one of your bedrooms. Perhaps it was the bedroom where your parents once lived. As you clean out the closet, which was filled with some of their old stuff, you notice something surprising. The back wall of the closet, behind the clothes, is not really a wall—it is actually an old door, which is painted shut. It is a small door, perhaps just large enough to enter.

With a little effort, you force the creaky door open and peer inside. A flight of stairs leads down into the darkness. You quickly go to find a flashlight, then switch it on and crouch to pass through the doorway. You cautiously descend the stairs into the darkness.

At the bottom of the stairway, you discover something that is difficult to absorb. Below the bedroom you were cleaning spreads a massive room, and its walls are the foundation for your entire house. The room seems to be filled with curious objects of every color and shape. As in Jobim's river, you can make out a stick, a stone, and a sliver of glass…

As you pass your beam over the room's unseen contents, you notice some things your parents never wanted to talk about. You also

2

In our early adulthood, we rarely notice we have been sitting on our family's old divan of understanding. When I was a young man, I spent much of my time talking about the religious ideas I had grown up with. In my family, we did not discuss our feelings, and we usually did not even admit we *had* feelings. It was much more acceptable to talk about ideas, especially religious ones. As I grew older, if anyone challenged my carefully defended position, I was quick to argue how my beliefs were more correct than others.

If ideas become our identity, then we are what we believe. We have become our own worldview. The stronger we identify with our couch, the more difficult it is for us to get up. When we are this comfortable, it seems unnecessary to explore any new, mysterious space within our interior...even if that space rests right below us.

This is how I lived in young adulthood. I had no curiosity for exploration of my personal space.

There are many ways of avoiding exploration. Any idea we are attached to can be an idea we hide behind. It is certainly possible to avoid our unexplored room by talking about religion (or politics or science, for that matter). We can be attached to lots of things in the upstairs.

A few years after I attended medical school, I was really attached to the science I had learned. I was certain about how some diseases ought to be treated. Back then, if I found someone who disagreed with me, I would argue my points about medical concepts all day; I would even hunt for scientific articles that proved me right. If there wasn't good science behind my opponent's idea, I was ready to dismiss it.

Defending ourselves can become a lonely task, especially if being religious or scientific is our way of avoiding our own interior. Living in the upstairs and keeping everything on an intellectual level might control unpleasantness for a while, but this kind of control makes it more difficult for us to really connect with one another as human beings. Eventually our couch just doesn't work anymore.

When we finally gain a glimpse of even *some* of the concealed stuff waiting in our unexplored room, we have gained a permanent, deeper viewpoint. We are off the couch for good. Once we taste the unseen reality of our unexplored room, we find ourselves becoming larger than the old ideas that kept us sitting. We begin to see ourselves and others with new perspective and compassion— and even with a little humor. The flat construct of life we were once certain of becomes three-dimensional.

Once we have discovered our unexplored room, we realize we have been sleepwalking. We may notice how fear, anger, or grief interfered with our lives and how our own emotions kept out of our reach the very things we wanted most. In future chapters, we will explore the personal treasure forgotten in our unexplored room. If we have never entered, we may be living in scarcity while we are actually in possession of unimagined abundance.

Intense personal pain can be misleading when it originates from concealed material. We all have a tendency to blame our worst pain on the ones we are with. We will explore this phenomenon as well. If we have never known about the unexplored room, then old traumas that hurt or frightened us long ago remain viable and may recur.

In exploring this room, we might discover the origin of our anger that bubbles up unexpectedly. We might also learn why we have attracted the very people we live with and why they seem to hurt us repeatedly.

What are the consequences of being unconscious of our room? Broken relationships can certainly be one. It is easy to misunderstand negative emotions generated within a relationship and miss the real origin of our hurt feelings. If we are confined to live upstairs, it may be hard for us to access the deeper parts of ourselves for a relationship. It is hard to respond on a heart level to the person we are with when we have never looked at our own issues. It is also more difficult to resonate with their pain or their joy.

Before I began to understand the material in my own unexplored room, I personally found it hard to stay connected in my primary relationship. Sustained relationships require a kind of heart connection, which is difficult to achieve when painful material keeps welling up from the basement.

After my third divorce, I had to admit there might be something wrong with me. I imagined therapy might fix me, so I found a therapist and told her my story: I had been in one relationship after another. Each had started with love and good intentions, and each had become too difficult and painful. No matter who I was with, I found myself eventually shutting down and withdrawing. My inability to stay attached had created a trail of fractured relationships.

She agreed there was something wrong with me. She asked me, "Does it ever feel like you pour all of yourself into a relationship as if it were a bucket, but your bucket is full of holes? Every time your bucket is filled up, all the water leaks out?"

My life was like this. I felt helpless and broken.

"Yes!" I replied. "So can you fix the holes? Will therapy plug the holes?"

She bluntly replied, "No." She paused. "You just have to stop putting water in the bucket!"

I found another therapist.

She was someone trapped in a useless metaphor. To her, I was just a bucket full of holes. If I lived inside her model of life, I would always view myself as someone who was broken. I would never be able to show up for a long-term relationship.

It's not that I don't sympathize with her cynicism—it's challenging to deal with clients who are suffering but are unready to work on their stuff. But these days, I have a different metaphor for myself and for others.

When I talk to someone who has had multiple failed relationships, I do not picture a bucket full of holes. Instead, I picture an unexplored room. And if I notice a little fear emerging around the prospect of doing work in this place, I remember my own journey. Each entry into the unexplored room is a small act of courage.

What does it feel like when the presence of our unexplored room becomes certain? Honestly, it might feel a little unsafe at first. Often, we first glimpse our unexplored room through illness, threatened death, or catastrophe. It might take a sense of desperation for us to open this door. Opening the door may involve saying hello to family secrets that have always remained unspoken. It may involve revisiting painful events we have wanted to forget. It may result in naming a difficult feeling or talking about where this feeling comes from. Entering this space can be scary.

If we are unconscious of having an unexplored room, then there are times when this material will climb upstairs and poke us, like an unwelcome visitor. We will talk more about this later. In my own relationships, it was common for me to be triggered when my partner expressed anger. My reaction of fear was usually disproportionate to the situation, because it came from my own unseen issues. These were fears that crept upstairs like a burglar, taking control of my response. I felt compelled to escape from my partner, and I didn't even know why.

When we experience unexplained anxiety, our feelings are often about concealed things from the unexplored room. This material can be a source of real stress that can even manifest as illness in the doctor's office. I have noticed it is not uncommon for patients to report real pain, real panic, and real shortness of breath as the results of underlying stress. In stress-related illness, our body's normal physical response to stress creates symptoms, and there is often no detectable medical cause for these. Stress-related illness produces a huge burden in our society in terms of medical care and expense, leading to lots of unnecessary medical testing and treatment. Prescriptions and surgery are both unsuccessful in relieving stress, because they do not open the door to the unexplored room.

If a doctor asks if sadness or anger might contribute to our complaint, our first reflex is to focus on our symptoms, because sadness and anger are internalized. Denial can be a cornerstone of stress-related illness.

This kind of scenario isn't limited to patients: I have struggled with stress at work and have known many medical colleagues and friends who have struggled, too. Stress can make it difficult for us to do our work and create connections with one another. If we are caregivers, stress can also make it hard to create connections with the people we are caring for.

Sometimes the origin of the stress is deeper than the surface details of our work. Sometimes the stress originates from something deeper than our job description, our hours, or our coworkers. Sometimes stress originates from a part of us that has been unexamined.

If we are caregivers, then things reside in our unexplored room that can interfere with our work. For example, sometimes we have lost a loved one to death in an untimely way. This loss can lead us to harbor the fear of death if we have not worked with our own material. If we have not processed our personal loss, then fear waits for us. When we are caring for someone with a terminal condition, our own hidden fears can surface. Our emotions can make it more difficult for us to prepare patients and their families for death with neutrality and acceptance.

If death is only an enemy living in our unexplored room, then we go to war anytime the threat of mortality surfaces. Sometimes war is vital, but sometimes this is the wrong battle to fight. If war with death is our only dynamic as caregivers, then we are predisposed to wage grim, expensive battles at the end of life by using difficult medical interventions with little chance of success. Consciousness of and peace with our own mortality comes through work in our unexplored room and has the capacity to change how we provide (and receive) care at the end of life.

Many of my colleagues have come to hate medical practice. When anger like this surfaces, it is often directed at the health-care system. This can be related to how doctors often work for large health-care companies now (instead of for themselves in private practice). It can also reflect the complex digitalization of health care, with the electronic medical record and all the stress that goes with it. Sometimes, their loss of love for medical practice is really a symptom of professional burnout, a phenomenon seen throughout modern culture. Burnout is defined as a loss of meaning in the workplace associated with exhaustion, but not relieved by rest.

Burnout in health care is associated with something described as "compassion fatigue," which occurs when it is no longer possible to feel empathy for those we are caring for. We sometimes use cynicism, sarcasm, and caustic humor to block our legitimate sense of grief and loss. Like the combat fatigue of soldiers, compassion fatigue may be a manifestation of work-related trauma, signaling an urgent need for a personal retreat. There are times when burnout points us toward grief work that waits in the unexplored room.

Unconsciousness of our unprocessed material numbs our perception. We fail to see ourselves or others clearly. If you have been out in the cold without adequate clothing, your hands and feet become numb. The lack of circulation from cold creates a painful numbness. Similarly, if you are caring for those with serious illness, the pain can be numbing. While it is true that drugs or alcohol may block out painful numbness, there are many other ways to escape. Painful numbness can also be escaped with sex, food, sports, workaholism, entertainment, religion, wealth, or even new relationships. Blotting out reality provides only a shallow relief.

When we come back inside from the cold and put our hands and feet into warm water, we first feel a burning pain as the circulation returns. But what follows is the flush of delicious sensation. Similarly, restoration of the circulation to our numb heart can also be painful at first.

What would ever lead us to do this uncomfortable work? It happens when the couch becomes uncomfortable, which can occur in many ways. If we pause and allow ourselves some silent space, some questions arise from our discomfort.

Sometimes the stress of work forces us to ask, "What am I really here to do?"

Sometimes a fractured relationship may prompt us to ask, "Why did this happen to me?"

Insurmountable loss or illness may encourage us to wonder, "What is my life really about?"

These questions illuminate the doorway of our unexplored room. But when we discover the door, we find a personal dilemma.

Passing through this doorway is an act of vulnerability. It means we are taking ownership of our own stuff; this is not someone else's doorway—entering the room means we own the door and what lies behind it. But vulnerability like this is not an act of weakness. Best-selling author and research professor Brené Brown has articulated clearly that there is profound strength to be found inside vulnerability. It is in the moments that we see our weakness, and even ask for help that we show the greatest inner strength.

Sometimes our work in the unexplored room begins by journaling, and sometimes the process will start with therapy. But our desire to heal and grow often leads us to the symbolic, experiential therapies described in this book.

As a physician and scientist, I have authored many scientific publications, but I now find myself intentionally writing a book that is not annotated with scientific references (although I *have* created an appendix for you at the end). The bottom line is this: A message from the mind reaches the mind, but a message from the heart reaches the heart. I am writing a message from my heart.

You may find yourself asking where the data and scientific proof are, for the value of such an internal expedition into the things we have avoided looking at. This is the kind of question that I have asked in my own professional life. For me, these are the questions that originate from a certain couch I have mentioned previously. Many of us have experienced a kind of "head learning" as we sat through PowerPoint presentations, taking notes in class. But this is not the kind of knowledge central to this book; we're entering a different domain of learning here.

There is a Buddhist tradition that warns, "Trust only that which is true, in your own experience." This is because experience is the most powerful teacher, and experience contrasts with the traditional lecture style of education in universities. Appreciation of experience has birthed the idea of the "reverse classroom" used in many universities and in medical education. In this style of teaching, lectures and reading are done outside of class time, which is reserved for interaction with the teacher and where real-life cases are experienced. In medical education, experience is now valued over lecture time, because students are likelier to internalize and retain the lesson's content on a deeper level. The work found inside the unexplored room also happens through experience.

There is a quality of human interaction that I think of as a "heart con-nection," which we will discuss later. Heart connection is not easily quantified by medical science, though it is possible to estimate our emotional state by measuring heart-rate variability during human activities. In the way I think of it, a heart connection is an intuitive event that tends to defy scientific study. We will discuss some good reasons for this. Even without any scientific measurement, most of us respond when we have experienced a soulful connection with someone.

Years before we married, my wife, Suzi, introduced me to a teach-er she loved and gave me one of his lectures to listen to. He was a psychology professor and a metaphysical speaker who was cre-ative and poetic. He spoke with power and certainty. But I was troubled when I listened to him, because I thought, *There is no data for what he is saying. How does he know that what he says is true?*

I had a conversation with Suzi about this later. I told her the teacher was interesting but that I struggled to listen to his ideas, because

I had no way of knowing what he said was true. Suzi's reply astounded me.

She asked, "Do you know that I love you?"

"Yes!" I answered, without thinking. "Of course I do."

Then she asked, "How do you know?" I was speechless. There was no data to answer her question. I could make a list of things she did and said, but that wasn't the point. I knew on a heart level that she loved me.

Her point was, of course, that there are different ways to know things. How we know something really matters. Sometimes we know things in our head because there is compelling data, and it makes sense. But there are other things we can know only with our hearts. When someone seems to be "following their heart," we often notice and even remark about it.

Heart-based action is the subject of countless books and movies and is also at the core of recovery programs for alcoholism and addiction. In twelve-step traditions, it is frequently repeated that each of the twelve steps begins with the same word: *We.*

In this tradition, it is commonly held that someone can read every book written on recovery and still fail to recover. It is widely held that "We" is the most essential element of recovery in all twelve-step traditions, because recovery is actually created through heart connections grown within the recovery community.

When a heart connection occurs, we all know something has happened. We can feel it. We are changed and touched. We feel differently about ourselves, and we feel differently about the person who connected with us.

As doctors, we are trained to be logical and knowledgeable scientists who analyze problems, and there are regular times when we need to be analytical. But over the years, I also have learned to connect with my heart when I am with patients. Sometimes, this means I might disclose something personal about myself. I try to reduce the power gradient between us. I look into their eyes. Sometimes, I consciously break the rules of "formal professional behavior," and if the moment is right, I may offer a hug. This is because I know a heart connection is where the deepest kind of healing occurs.

When I connect with patients in this way, I have found that even a minor word or two can powerfully shift the way someone sees their life. With this kind of connection, I have also found deeper meaning in my work.

Within each of us, there resides the same concealed stairway leading to a space filled with the unseen we have discarded and rejected. It is filled with the things we thought we would never need and the things our parents and society told us were unacceptable. This is where our pain is hidden away. But it is also a space that contains incredible potential.

When we begin to work with the material from our unexplored room, we change. This change completely shifts how we show up for the people around us. When we recognize our own issues, we see those around us with new eyes.

∽

Reflection

At the end of each chapter, I will offer a reflection to help you to sit with, and drop more deeply into the ideas we have explored. A quiet moment in a quiet place will work best for experiencing some of what you have just read.

Find a place to sit comfortably with your feet on the floor and your back straight, if possible. Breathe in deeply, and then exhale fully. Do this again as you notice your body relaxing. As you feel ready, let your imagination emerge.

Imagine you are working in a closet in your house. Imagine finding the margins of a door at the back of the closet. Imagine pushing on the door and feeling it break free. It creaks open. Imagine peering down the stairway into your unexplored room with the narrow beam of a flashlight.

Notice your feelings on the stairway. Do you sense a little anxiety? Do you feel a little resistance? Do you taste the possibility of adventure?

What could be hidden here for you?
Were there things that were never spoken of as you grew up?
Were there emotions that were not allowed in your family?
Were there parts of yourself that were not welcome in your family?
Did you ever have dreams or aspirations that you had to put away?
Does there seem to be an emotional texture to your unexplored room?

Say hello to any feelings that present themselves here.

This is a wonderful, magical space that belongs to you. This is a space you carry with you everywhere. This is a space that comes to visit you...

Breathe in the feeling, and then let it out. Breathe in deeply, and then exhale fully. Open your eyes when you are ready to come back to the room where you are sitting.

Chapter Two
The Heart Connection

Oh people stay…just a little bit longer…
We wanna play…just a little bit more

—Jackson Browne

In his song, "The Load-Out/Stay," I think singer-songwriter Jackson Browne created the first standing ovation musicians have ever given to their audience. In this classic song, the speaker/singer is a road-weary musician who will be in either Chicago or Detroit tomorrow night. He doesn't remember which, because they do "so many shows in a row." The only thing he and his fellow musicians look forward to is that moment when the curtains come up and they are back onstage, connecting with their audience. He sings to the audience, "Please stay, just a little bit longer…"

What Browne is really talking about in the song is the heart connection musicians sometimes feel with their audience. It is a magical thing, and I have experienced it.

I remember playing keyboards in a neo-soul band with Buffalo's singer, Nikki Hicks, and sax player Will Holton a few years ago. It was late on a summer evening at a club called Le Metro, and all the windows were open. We were covering an Anita Baker tune. As we played, I noticed a man and a woman pass each other on the side-walk outside. They could hear our music and felt it, in the moment. They seemed to be strangers, but they looked at each other, looked at us, and smiled. They started dancing with each other, right there on the sidewalk outside, as we played on. The crowd didn't want us to quit, and Will played the solo of his life, from somewhere in his heart. We were all connected to one another in that club. This is the kind of moment musicians live for.

I played professional jazz keyboard in New York clubs for several decades. Hanging out with musicians, you get to hear all kinds of solos. Some soloists are technically accomplished, with crazy riffs and flashy runs. The crowd might be impressed, but the musicians in the back all just shrug their shoulders, roll their eyes, and say, "Next."

But every now and then, someone would come along who was not trying to impress anybody with their technique. He or she would take a solo and play creatively from the heart. The pain would come up. The joy. Tears would well up. It was real, and everyone could feel it. That is the solo we all lived for. The maxim among the musi-cians I played with was, "If it ain't got soul, it don't matter."

When someone performs something musical or creates something artful and does it with soul, he or she reaches into the unexplored room. As they play, or paint, or sing, or dance, they are drawing from this unconscious place where untouchable pain simmers and joy shimmers. And as we listen to them or observe their work, something happens within us. We resonate. When a comedian tells a story and we laugh, it is because she has pulled back the curtain to show us an unseen truth about ourselves. We laugh because we recognize it as our own. When an artist performs with soul, he or she will touch the joy and sadness we hide from ourselves.

This is why in the arts we admire one quality above technical brilliance: heart. When the artist performs from his or her heart, we find ourselves feeling as though we know them. Robin Williams achieved this when he played Dr. Patch Adams. Here was a man who created heart connections with his patients and colleagues through humor. In this movie character, Williams eventually finds himself at odds with his teachers, because modern medicine, like most of modern society, has a long tradition of avoiding heart connections.

In the nineteenth century, Sir William Osler told his medical students to cultivate "a judicious measure of obtuseness" when dealing with patients. In other words: be detached.

I felt the effects of this teaching in some of my own medical training. In medical science, we are taught that the treatment of disease should be based only on scientific evidence. Diseases are analyzed objectively, and in order to do this, we imagine that all illnesses are distinct entities. They are something separate from the person who is sick.

This teaching has a side effect. If we objectify disease, our patients can be reduced to "a case." A heart case. A lung case. A hip fracture. On top of this, caregivers are then taught to adhere to "evidence-based guidelines" for the treatment of every case.

Greg Loewen

There are no guidelines to recommend that doctors create a heart connection with their patients. Some of us try to do it anyway, out of instinct. Most of us were taught that we needed to be detached, so we don't lose our "objectivity."

Science, medicine, and much of modern society have idealized "being objective." Science has become the powerful lens that turns every object into a thing that can be studied. It has changed the way we understand disease and has transformed the universe of medical treatment. Through science, we can now cure diseases that once were incurable. Sometimes. There are also times we struggle with human problems, which are more complex.

In health care, the problem is almost always more than the disease. Usually, the problem is really a patient who happens to have the disease. Often, the disease is not the cause but the effect. The illness may evolve through a lack of self-care or by self-inflicted harm. Sometimes the sick person has so much despair that he or she refuses the simplest treatment for something completely fixable. Sometimes treatment is hindered by an angry or unwell family. Human illness is more complicated than a science experiment.

Osler also said, "It is more important to know what kind of patient has the disease than it is to know what kind of disease the patient has."

I would add that it is easier to know what kind of patient has the disease if we have created a heart connection with him or her. This issue affects us all, especially when we are sick. If we want to understand someone, then we have to connect with them.

Science teaches that data is truth; however, if you were to attend a scientific medical conference with me, you would see there are many ways to interpret data. And lots of argument about the data. Data is not truth, exactly; it leads us to an understanding of something, and that understanding can make reliable predictions sometimes.

In many work spaces, we are pressured to make decisions based on data alone. But data-driven decisions (for doctors or for anyone else) do not take intuition into account. Decisions like these cannot honor our values or our emotions.

Being human is about something greater than data. From Plato to Immanuel Kant, philosophers have affirmed that our human experience unfolds in many arenas, not just in one. One way of saying this is that in life, yes, there is truth, but there are also goodness and beauty.

Ken Wilber writes about this and suggests that in our modern era, when we say *truth*, we are really referring to something that can be measured. In other words, in our culture, truth means science. Anything can be studied, and when we study something, that thing becomes an *it*. *Truth* in this light means we have objectified the thing we have studied. Truth is the place where scientists live and work and where we understand and interpret data.

In contrast, Wilber points out that there are other vital aspects of being human. Another area, called *beauty* by the Greeks, is found in music, arts, and spirituality. When something is beautiful to us, then it is personal. Beauty is subjective. What I find to be beautiful may be quite ugly to you. There is no foolproof test for beauty.

Meaning and spirituality are also aspects of beauty. What I find to be meaningful may be quite different from what you find to be important or moving. Artists and spiritual leaders all find themselves working with beauty to create meaning.

Wilber points out that the realm of goodness is a third area of human life. Goodness happens when we relate to one another. If something is good, it is because we have experienced compassion or fairness. Society perceives goodness through shared intuition. We have laws that attempt to establish what is good and fair. Judges, lawyers, law enforcement, and administrators all use the law and their intuition when they decide what is fair and good.

Whenever we experience a heart connection with someone, it is because we sense all these qualities. If we really connect to them, it is because we sense that they are compassionate and authentic. We can measure what is true, but there is no scientific test for the good or the beautiful. This is why a heart connection is hard to measure.

In the way I am using the word *heart*, it means our emotional life. This muscular, electrical organ in the center of our chest is closely connected to our feelings. It is well-documented that under severe stress, a young, healthy heart can fail. When a catastrophic release of stress hormones occurs, it can result in a kind of heart attack.

This uncommon form of heart attack is known as Takotsubo syndrome, which is a reference to the Japanese "octopus trap." On an echocardiogram picture of someone with Takotsubo, videos of the heart show it ballooning up like an octopus, caught in a trap from below. Takotsubo syndrome happens in younger people with normal coronary arteries, who are under severe stress. In a poetic sense, it is said that individuals who die from this have died from "a broken heart."

In the hospital ICU, stress is routinely monitored with the heart rate and measurement of blood pressure. It is also possible to measure the physical manifestations of stress through the variability of the heart rate. The Heart Math Institute and others have used heart-rate variability to teach relaxation techniques to people who are stressed. There are valid reasons to use the word *heart* for our emotional life.

What would it be like to be a scientist, who also creates heart connections with people? What would it be like to work in a place where everyone kept an awareness of truth, along with goodness and beauty? This ideal has become a touchstone for service industries, when they ask customers, "How well did we connect with you?" We are all being surveyed. This is also true for those of us who are in medical practice right now.

These days, many of our patients are asked to complete a questionnaire after they visit us in the clinic. They are asked how satisfied they were with us. They are asked if we listened well. They are asked if we explained things well. They are asked if we spent enough time with them. They are asked if they would come back to see us again.

The results of these questionnaires are turned into something called an "exit interview" score, and this is used to rate us as caregivers. It is a report card for doctors.

Sometimes we doctors might make the right diagnosis and even might prescribe the right medication, but if we seem busy, detached, or arrogant, then we will probably be faced with a low score.

A new twist to this measurement is that doctors and hospitals are now being paid based on their scores. Because of this, hospitals are starting to worry about exit interviews. Some of my colleagues have imagined their scores are a measure of whether they ordered enough tests or gave out enough pain medications, but I don't think it's that simple.

I think these exit interviews measure whether we have connected with one another. They ask if we have connected with our hearts. Did we connect with our audience? They want to know if we played with soul.

If we doctors imagine we can meet the needs of our patients with nothing more than knowledge, then we will take a hit ourselves. Many of us have become unhappy, as we look at practice with this point of view. The rate of burnout exceeds 50 percent in my profession (pulmonary/critical care) and in emergency medicine. According to one survey, 34 percent of practicing doctors plan to leave their field. Author Dike Drummond writes that burnout is never solved by rest, in any amount. If you listen carefully to someone who is burned out, you actually might even hear him or her say, "My heart just isn't in it anymore." What a telling diagnosis.

Christina Maslach has done pioneering work to understand burnout in all kinds of workplaces. She surveyed work environments and workers over several decades, and she found patterns that will consistently produce a "burnout environment." As you might expect, work overload and a sense of unfairness always foster burnout. Other environmental triggers found by Maslach included inadequate control over how to do our jobs and unreasonable recurring criticism from employers. Another thing that promotes burnout is value conflict. If we are asked to do something we feel conflicted about (as happened in recent banking scandals), then we feel stress.

I experienced something like this in a common situation. Small private practices are not created only to treat patients who are sick. They are also small businesses. In order to survive, they have to be. The unfortunate truth is that the things that make a business healthy (like ordering more tests or doing more surgeries) are not necessarily the same things that will make a patient healthy.

When I left my work as a researcher and a teacher to join a small private-practice group, I was in for a bit of a shock. I learned we were expected to be extremely conscious of our own monthly financial productivity. As a medical specialist, this meant counting how many tests I ordered and how many procedures I did. In order to make my salary or to receive any bonuses (which I never achieved), there was an unspoken incentive for me to do more tests and perform more procedures. This pressure was a conflict for me, as it is for many, when medical care is a business. I needed to find a way out.

I left the practice to work as an employee of a faith-based hospital with a mission to provide care to the poor and vulnerable. The uninsured and the homeless were welcomed in my new office, and I was given a stable salary. There was a small bonus offered to all employed physicians, but it wasn't based on the number of tests we ordered or the number of procedures we did. It was based on our exit interviews. I was paid extra for connecting with my patients. My stress evaporated when I worked for a company whose values were in alignment with my own.

The most common and most reliable predictor of burnout was something else. Maslach described "the breakdown of the workplace community." This is another way of saying "loss of connection." She found this to be true in any kind of workplace. And the loss of connection wasn't only between coworkers. It was between workers and those they served. One of the end results of the electronic age is that doctors are often expected to type on the computer while talking to their patients. How is it possible to connect heart-to-heart with someone while you are typing on a computer?

Every day when I am in my clinic, I set an intention to create a heart connection with everyone I see. Sometimes it isn't easy, because like everyone else, I have difficult patients, and sometimes my staff and I have difficult days too. I deal with death and dying, and all the fear and unhappiness that go with it, on a daily basis. But on a good day, my patients leave feeling differently about their disease and may even feel differently about themselves.

On most days, I find a lot of meaning and happiness in my work. If I filled out an exit interview about my patients, I would say, "I would love to see you again!" I could be like Jackson Browne singing, "Stay, just a little bit longer!"

This could be true of everyone's work space, especially when work involves contact with people. If we can find a way of connecting with others in our work space, it transforms how we feel about what we are doing. Connection *charges* our work with meaning, and it is at the core of job satisfaction. Maslach teaches that the opposite of burnout is engagement. Consultants are hired by industry to repair burnout by cultivating connections between coworkers and between workers and their clients. We live in a society that is willing to pay for heart connections at work.

There is a kind of "medical healing" that depends completely on a heart connection. Deepak Chopra describes healing as a restoration of wholeness and points out that *wholeness* and *healing* both come from the same root word in Sanskrit. If healing is viewed in this way, then healing is about listening and teaching. It is not just about diagnosis and treatment.

Medical healing is about connecting with people and helping them to understand and reframe their lives. It is about restoring wholeness. Healing is about offering a new way to see illness and a new way to see ourselves. Yes, once in a while we write a prescription or do a procedure. But healing is infinitely more complex than this and requires a deeper connection.

Healing requires a temporary umbilical cord between the healer and the patient. Even though there may be an exchange of data, there also is a connection. When I have been sick in the past, I have noticed my own desire for something more from those who cared for me. We are vulnerable when we are sick. When I am in a place of vulnerability, it is possible for a caregiver to expose himself or herself a little in a careful way. Everyone has been sick. Everyone knows what it is like. If caregivers can disclose even a little of their humanity, our interaction becomes infinitely safer. Trust is created.

Not long ago, I was hospitalized with chest pain, which led to a CT scan of the chest. I learned in the ED that I had an enlargement, or aneurism of my aorta, with narrowing of my aortic valve. I was panicked. I knew major heart surgery would eventually be necessary. Imagine how I felt as I sat trembling in my bed, when my new cardiologist sat down next to me, and patted me on the knee. She looked me kindly in the eyes and said, "Don't worry. I have the same thing as you. You are gonna be OK."

In one instant, my panic melted. His self-disclosure had created a connection with me. I received a rapid infusion of hope. I immediately felt differently about my own illness. His openness and kindness are part of what led me to write this book. This is a kind of heart connection that has extraordinary power in any workplace.

Is there a downside of connecting with your heart? Are there any risks?

Many years ago, when I was an intern on a rotation for the gastroenterology service, I found myself developing a friendship with a patient I will call Helen. Helen was a warmhearted, humorous elderly lady who was suffering from inflammatory bowel disease. She required hospitalization for IV steroids and fluids. I remember sitting on her bed and conversing with her as I made my rounds. I really liked her.

One night when I was on call, Helen's condition suddenly deteriorated, and she was transferred to the ICU. She was septic and was bleeding from her colon. We did all the usual interventions to save her with antibiotics, transfusions, and critical-care monitoring. Late in the night, despite all our efforts, her heartbeat stopped when I was at her bedside. I called for help, got up on her bed, and began CPR. This was my first glimpse of death as a young man. I was twenty-four at the time, and I felt such grief. I remember doing compressions on her chest as I wept. As the team quickly gathered at the bedside, one of the nurses saw my distress, and she kindly took over CPR. Helen died that night.

Psychologists caution about this scenario. Empathy means we have connected so deeply that we share someone's suffering. When we empathize like this, we are often feeling our own material from our unexplored room. I think this is precisely the dilemma Sir William Osler was worried about when he recommended "professional detachment." In this sense, he was right. I will have clouded judgment if I am overcome by my own emotions.

When someone's heartbeat stops in the hospital, a "code" or a "Code Blue" is called on the loudspeakers overhead. The code team runs from every hallway and assembles in the room to begin CPR and give IV medications as they try to save the person's life. As an intensivist pulmonologist over the years, I have led the code team hundreds of times.

When a patient's life is in jeopardy, there is a sense of danger that is already in the room. If the person leading the code team is also in fear (or anger), the entire team is drawn into this emotional space. Team members are more prone to make mistakes when this happens.

As I progressed in my training and in my own personal development, I found that running a good code is managing a crisis. It requires more than a mastery of the problem at hand. To start with, it requires a neutral curiosity. It is crucial to start with questions: What is trying to happen here? What is the overall process that led to this critical event? What is the next step to take? These are questions from the realm of science. But there are other equally important things to be aware of in a crisis.

Emotion and intuition actually augment our ability to process data in a crisis. It isn't necessary for emotions to control our judgment, if we are able to view our own emotions as information. This is because there is a profound difference between being afraid and noticing when a sense of fear arises. If something doesn't seem right to us, this is important information. Noticing a sense of my own fear can actually lead to a corrected diagnosis in medicine—or anywhere else.

If something doesn't seem right, my intuition can be a guide, and being in a crisis with an awareness of my heart can actually save someone's life.

Everyone's best performance in a crisis is related to clear communication, and this improves when you connect with the coworkers around you. Code teams function best if there is a sense of easeful command and gratitude for any tasks that are performed well. Teamwork and communication have become part of routine teaching for Advanced Cardiac Life Support. But emotional awareness is also needed, because all members perform at their peak in a crisis if they are alert, comfortable, and appreciated. A centered leader who is in touch with his own heart creates that sort of environment.

This is true, too, for engineers, teachers, parents, and political leaders. We all must face a crisis, and we all must lead sometimes.

Goodness and beauty by themselves are not enough to manage a crisis. But truth isn't enough, either. To be most effective in any crisis, we need all our humanity. We need to integrate our hearts into our work space.

Another risk of making heart connections has been described in psychiatry as "countertransference." Freud coined this term for when a therapist finds his own emotions (from the past) are triggered by a patient's interaction with him. The classic case of countertransference occurs if a therapist falls in romantic love with his client. This is a real danger, because romance is a powerful illusion. Romantic relationships are forbidden between therapists and their clients, because of the invisible power gradient therapy rests upon. The therapist has power, and the client does not. It is not an equal relationship.

Countertransference is an illusion that originates from our unexplored room. This is an illusion that can drive us off the road if we do not recognize it.

Countertransference is not limited to romantic love. It can happen in any situation where we care for others. In my case, as I look back, I think I experienced countertransference with Helen. As she died, I was impaired by grief. But it probably wasn't just grief for Helen, really. It was a deeper grief that came from issues I hadn't worked on yet.

The problem with my temporary illusion is that I became a person who needed comforting, instead of being able to show up in a professional way to do my work.
This is a real risk of heart connection anywhere.

When illusions like this happen to us in normal life, we call them "emotional triggers." Emotional triggers occur every day and are a part of the normal tapestry of long-term relationships. When we are intensely attracted to (or irritated by) our partner, it usually springs from a similarity between them and a parent or a significant person in our formative years. Anytime we allow ourselves to connect with our hearts, we open ourselves to the risk of being triggered.

My wife's mentor asks a rhetorical question sometimes: "What do you get when you rescue a damsel in distress?"

Her answer is "a distressed damsel," though it works with either gender. Whenever we come to someone else's rescue in a relationship, we wind up with a person who needs to be rescued. If rescue is the foundation of our relationship, then we are codependent. When our partner in a relationship is stuck in addiction, we are stuck too. Down the stairs in our unexplored room, their illness is really our way of trying to fix our own unresolved issues.

Codependency is often mentioned when someone has loved an alcoholic spouse, but it is also the nature of a "wounded healer" too. Codependency can motivate anyone on a mission to save the world. If internal pain drives my work to help others, then I will always have emotional triggers that *interfere* with my work. There is no good substitute for working on our stuff.

Psychiatrists, psychologists, and therapists are required to go through their own therapy in order to complete their training. Medical doctors are generally not required to do this yet, but perhaps someday this will change. And what would the world be like, if we all were required to become familiar with our own interiors? No matter what we do in life, we eventually need to work on our stuff.

We need access to all our humanity if we want to connect with others. It is a lot riskier to connect with others if our unexplored rooms are unfamiliar territory. This internal work is what brings meaning to our work space. Work on our stuff brings grounded stability and creates extraordinary leadership skills. It is what helps us to understand ourselves and others.

This is exactly what happened to me. Working on my stuff changed the way I connected to everyone. I began to take a new solo in my life, and I played with soul. Everyone noticed.

Reflection

Create a quiet moment in a quiet place. Sit comfortably, with your feet on the floor and your back straight, if you can. Breathe in deeply and then exhale fully. Do this again, as you notice your body begin to relax.

As your body relaxes, let yourself become light and buoyant. Allow yourself to drift lazily above your life…

Do you notice any heart connections that have been meaningful to you?
Do you see any areas of your life that feel stressful or isolated?
Do you sense a hunger for some kind of meaning in your work space?
Have you ever faced an illness or challenge when you felt vulnerable?
Have you ever faced a crisis where your emotions were overwhelming?

Merely notice what comes up for you, without judgment.

Now, look toward your unexplored room. Imagine the unseen or rejected parts of yourself…
This is a place that can offer you wholeness…
This is the place where you will find soulfulness…

Could exploration of your interior be what you are ready for?

Breathe in deeply and then exhale fully. Open your eyes when you are ready to come back to the room where you are sitting.

Chapter Three

Enough

Who wants to know what desperate is?
Who wants to buy what's broken?

—DAVID CROSBY

I used to quote a Steve Martin comic routine when I would give my story as a speaker for AA meetings. In his stand-up monologue years ago, Martin described a new (imaginary) drug he liked to take. Instead of "getting high," he would take the drug to "get small." He relays his experience of driving while "small" and being pulled over by the police. The officers came up to the window of his car and asked, "Sir, are you driving 'small'?"

He cried out in defense, "No! I'm tall! I'm tall!"

In Martin's routine, the police order him to step out of the car. Instead of asking him to walk a straight line, they measure his height. He is arrested for DWS.

It was funny to me twenty-two years ago, probably because it felt a little true.

Getting small is actually what happened to me. Predictably. If you ever read the "big book" of AA, in the second half of the book you will find scores of first-person stories that tell how each alcoholic got sober. The third story in this section is about the first alcoholic to get sober in Chicago's early AA group, and he describes where the traditional "twelve steps" of spiritual recovery came from. This writer notes that when AA first started, there were not twelve steps. There were only three. He then makes a seminal point for all recovery programs, and points out that, back then, the first step of AA didn't even mention the word *alcohol*.

In order to find recovery, the first step one must take was only two words: *Complete deflation* (of the ego)—getting small. When I first read this, I probably sounded a little like Seinfeld as I wondered, "What's up with that?"

I would have argued back then that everyone needs a healthy, robust ego to get clean and sober. I personally needed a strong ego in order to become a doctor and learn to operate on someone's lungs. Or to be a psychiatrist. Or to even get in to medical school. It also seemed to me that anyone would certainly need a healthy ego to be a businessman, a judge, a lawyer, a cop, or a teacher. Or to parent a child. And it takes a lot of ego strength to be any kind of creative artist. Or to be anything. The fact is, we all need a certain amount of ego strength to just live. Right?

Before I got sober, I played in a band called Mr. B and Company. The bandleader played guitar and harmonica, and we covered R and B tunes by Lou Rawls. One night, the band played in the basement of a church. It turned out that this was a gig for an AA party. There was laughter, soft drinks, and food, and it was a lot of fun. Halfway through the gig, we stopped playing, and Mr. B announced that the band was taking a break, so everyone could go upstairs for an AA meeting. Mr. B asked if I wanted to come upstairs with him and the rest of the band. I replied, "No thanks," and they all smiled at me. I distinctly remember thinking, *Thank God that there's something like AA out there for all of those poor bastards.*

A few short years later, I found myself attending my first AA meeting up in Rochester, Minnesota. This was when it dawned on me that I was actually one of the poor bastards I had felt sorry for.

When I first joined AA, I learned it was started by Bill W. and Dr. Bob, both of whom were dead when I joined in 1983. I thought, *This is great. There is room at the top for me.* My sponsor would have smiled.

I was in for a little reorientation. I was surprised to learn, for example, that AA has no president. No CEO. But it had lots of plain old members. There is plenty of room, but all the room is at the bottom.

My greatest reorientation occurred when I first sat down at a table in an AA discussion meeting. We sat in a circle. There was no hierarchy. We introduced ourselves one by one. I was no longer Dr. Loewen. I was no longer a specialist, a scientist, or a professor. I was compelled to announce my new identity, just like everyone else: "Hi. My name is Greg. I am an alcoholic."

The group answered in unison: "Hi, Greg!"

I detested admitting this about myself in public. In order to avoid the uncomfortable self-identification, I came to meetings late and left early. I stayed at the back of the room and went only to speaker meetings, where I could listen without having to introduce myself as an alcoholic. I found meetings that only doctors went to. I went to the "critically anonymous" meeting for professional athletes that my psychiatrist had created. I found lots of ways to protect my ego from a deep truth I would eventually get.

A few years later, and a few relapses later, my disease looked a little different to me. In Bob Dylan's words, it wasn't dark yet, but it was getting there. A few of my druggy friends had died from my disease. I had a few close calls of my own. I saw my personal and professional lives crumbling along the edges with each relapse. I was finally becoming afraid. It gently dawned on me: I actually had a lot in common with those people in AA meetings. My life did not restart until the last of my defenses fell.

These days, when I coach men, one of the first things I tell them is this: "Inside desperation is a gift. The gift is called—dramatic pause—*willingness*."

When I finally was given the gift of desperation, I was willing to get small.

When willingness finally surfaced in my life, you could see my behavior change. I actually found my own AA sponsor. My sponsor, Doug, suggested I go to ninety meetings in ninety days, four times a year. I was never great at math, so I just went to a meeting every day. For many years. I found a home AA group that I never missed.

I sat at the AA meeting tables, where I listened and I shared. I became a real part of the process.

Years later, I would tell those who I sponsored in AA that recovery is like a river. If you sit at the river's edge on the bank and dangle your feet in the water, you will always be in the same place at the end of the day. Alternatively, you can take a chance. You can jump out into the current and see where it takes you. When I finally was ready to jump into the river, I began to move forward.

After a few years of recovery, I moved up the ladder of achievement in AA. I was given a key to the church basement. I became the official coffee maker. I would get there early, set up the tables, make the coffee, and get everything ready for the meeting. I was usually all by myself when I set up the meeting. It was a quiet, joyous, humble gift of service. From grade school to the end of fellowship, I had spent over twenty-six years in education. I was a real expert. And now, I was a beginner, making coffee. You could almost hear the hiss as air escaped from my inflated ego. As it hissed out, something else became clear. I didn't have to do much in order to feel valuable. I only had to show up. Just like everyone else.

There's a clip from the movie *Sunshine Cleaning* that I love. A school-age boy named Oscar is riding in a pickup truck between his mother and his aunt. He asks his mother, "What is a bastard?"

She winces. "Why do you ask?"

"Jeremy said I was a bastard. What does that mean?"

His mom flinches as she feels the shameful truth behind his question. She is unable to even answer, but on the other side of the pickup, the boy's aunt quickly volunteers, "It just means your mom wasn't married when she had you. It's no big deal. In a couple of years, you're gonna find it's a free pass to cool. You'll probably start a band called 'Bastard Son.' Use it to impress the chicks. Trust me, the whole bastard thing…it's working for you."

The boy's face brightens.
Maybe this wasn't gonna be so bad after all.

Getting small changed the way I thought about those poor alcoholic bastards. But the odd thing about it is, my deflation eventually felt good. It felt good to join the rest of humanity. It felt good to be part of a home group. It felt good to begin to connect with the people at the tables. I began to feel value, as an ordinary person with no labels attached. And I realized my inflated picture of myself had prevented me from connecting to anyone. An inflated ego is a pretty lonely way to live.

Ego is not really who I am. It is a (false) idea of who I am. Ego is what I tell myself and what I try to tell you about me too. It is a slide show I want to project to everyone. Sometimes ego or "persona" is described as a mask. It is a mask that gets in our way as we get older. I used to tell myself (and you) that I was an important doctor, scientist, and professor. And a really good husband and father. And a masterful keyboard player. Why did I need these identities so badly? Some voice was coming from the center of my unexplored room—a voice that said I was worthless.

Worthlessness is at the core of all our secrets and abuse. Whenever we abuse anything, whether it is food, drugs, alcohol, relationships, sex, or power, we are only trying to medicate our internal sense of worthlessness. We are not enough.

You might not relate to my story of an overinflated ego. This is because sometimes our masks are not grandiose at all. Sometimes our ego projects a picture that is *less* than what we really are. This is a different kind of mask, but it is still a mask. If we have been beaten down by life and take a defeated view of ourselves, we are still rooted in feeling unworthy. Being a victim is about feeling unworthy. It is a paradox that abusers and victims both struggle with the same emptiness at their core.

If we feel beaten down when we discover our unexplored room's door, then something tells us we do not deserve to do this work. From our unexplored room we hear, "You are not enough..."

Suzi experienced sexual wounding at a very young age, and she grew up in fear. As an adult, she remained in abusive relationships, because she didn't feel worthy of anything better. She learned to stay small on purpose, in order to avoid more injury.

Coincidentally, Suzi's transformation began the same year I began my own recovery, over one thousand miles away. As she struggled with depression, she realized she was no longer OK with merely surviving. She was done with victim energy. She began to see herself as a person who could gain power over her life. She got up from her upstairs couch and entered her unexplored room by starting therapy.
She became empowered.

Empowerment and ego deflation are really two sides of the same coin, which buys us transformation. Both empowerment and deflation require us to see ourselves differently. When Suzi became empowered, she saw herself as enough. When I became deflated and released all those titles I hid behind, I began to see myself as enough too. If I wanted to survive, I had to be ordinary. As my ego shrank, my willingness grew.

My shrinking ego slowly changed something else about me. Once, on a psychiatry rotation years before, my attending physician had pointed to a doctor in the hospital cafeteria and whispered to me that this man was an alcoholic in recovery. I remember feeling sorry for him. I imagined how broken he must be. Sympathy is one feature of a robust ego.

But now, because of the gift of deflation, my response is completely different when I see someone with my disease. In the words of Ram Das, I say to myself, "I am that, too."

When I was on rounds in the intensive-care unit a few years ago, I remember caring for a young woman who had been admitted for a drug overdose. She was an addict. I heard the residents on our service making disparaging remarks like, "We can get her through this overdose, but she will be back next week with another one."

I gently tried to teach them that this woman had a disease she could actually recover from. I didn't look down on her, and I didn't feel sorry for her either. I looked down and saw myself in that bed. I also imagined she might someday be like me, with over twenty years of recovery. This is the powerful change of perspective that comes from getting small. Smallness makes a hope shot visible.

Once, in my first year of recovery, I showed up in an AA meeting after a fight with my daughters' mother. It was my turn to have my daughters on a Saturday morning, but their mother had made other plans. We argued. The tone escalated. I found myself pushing her aside to get to the kids, and she fell backward. She threatened to call the police. I left their house hurt, humiliated, and enraged. I didn't drink though. I went straight to a meeting.

At the meeting, when it was my turn, I described how humiliated I felt about what had just happened. I shared that I was afraid of relapsing. I was hurt and angry and embarrassed. I was in pain. We went around the table, and each person at the table shared their story about whatever was going on in their life. As the circle neared the end, an old, heavyset alcoholic in the back row looked at me and shared the words I will never forget.

He said, "Every time I have ever been in a fight with someone, it has always been about my ego. I come here to get small."

In that moment, the lights came on for me. I could see how my inflated ego had blown up my life. I went to my kids' house with an inflated image of myself as a great father, doing a cool-kid activity. I was so attached to my image that I couldn't be in the present moment. I couldn't see that something else was happening with my kids and their mom at that moment. I couldn't see that their change in plans wasn't even about me.

How important was my image of being an ideal dad? Did I really need to hold on to this and create drama for everyone? I thought about how my own ego had impaired me as a partner. It was starting to become clear that my ego might not be helping me to live with others. More deflation. *Hiss…*

For me, deflation led me to the small door of my unexplored room. Our arrival here comes in many ways. Sometimes it comes after a serious illness, an addiction, or the loss of a loved one. Sometimes it comes from a lost job or a lost marriage. Sometimes it can even come from a poor grade on a paper or a letter of rejection. Sometimes it comes after an embarrassing scandal. Sometimes it comes as a professional defeat, a botched presentation, or a flawed performance. But shedding our mask is a common, shared human experience. If we are ready, this is what reveals the doorway leading downward into our unknown interior.

Early in life, most of us are taught about who we are, and we eventually begin to believe a story about ourselves. Our narrative is often similar to the one our parents told us. Or if we react to their version, we might make it into something quite the opposite of what we were told. But either way, the story is about how we picture ourselves. This image is what becomes our ego. It is a normal and changing concept of who we are and who we will become. But when catastrophe strikes, our old story no longer fits.

In the tradition of recovery, we have a name for our self-inflated narratives. They are what we call "terminal uniqueness." These inflated stories are fatal for those of us with the disease of addiction, because they isolate us. If we fail to see what we have in common with one another, we die. But the ego deflation of recovery forces us to see others who have suffered in the same way as we have.

We learn that it is lifesaving to become ordinary. Ordinary is far from being boring, and it is the price we pay to become authentic.

I grew up in a religious subculture. Both my parents were very devout and taught at religious schools. Our tribe was pretty conservative, and among other things, they enthusiastically eschewed all alcohol use. I remember sitting in a restaurant in Portland, Oregon, with my parents when I was a kid. The waitress accidentally brought my dad a beer.

My mother was distraught. "Mike, get rid of it! Call her back right now! You are going to get fired!"

Our tribe's concept of "sin" included any alcohol use.
There was a teaching that went like this: "If you use alcohol, it is your choice. Sin is always a choice. Alcohol use is a sin. Therefore, if you are an alcoholic…"
Well, you can draw the conclusion.

Which of course I did.
I was a sinner.
I was quite familiar with the shame around alcohol use.
I had my first beer when I was twenty-one, and by age twenty-five, I was in treatment.

Let me interject here that this chapter is not really about alcoholism or drug addiction. It is about becoming authentic. If we start to see the doorway to our unexplored room, it is because we have shown up in a new identity. For example, most of my patients never imagined they would have cancer. But then one day, they suddenly became part of an exclusive club that, as Gilda Radner once observed, "You would prefer to not be a member of."

The shock of illness, divorce, or major loss makes us eligible for these exclusive clubs, where membership might even bring up a little embarrassment. Here was my first lesson in authenticity: at the AA meeting, I discovered that I belonged here, exactly like everyone else.

We have lived with societal shame for alcoholism (or any addictive behavior), but the disease model is a better way of viewing any human struggle (like victimhood, for example). One great advance of addiction medicine is the reframing of alcoholism (and other conditions) as illnesses. When I began to see that this part of myself was only a disease, my self-condemnation evaporated.

Picturing our internal struggles as illnesses allows room for self-compassion. And self-compassion is the hallmark of every spiritual tradition. Self-compassion is not some kind of "positive thinking." Instead, real feelings of compassion for the self will magically surface when we physically perform an act of self-care.

One of my first acts of self-care happened when I began therapy. This kind of self-care continued with every other workshop or activity described in my story. I found that each of my actions of kindness released feelings of worthlessness that had persisted in my interior. Personal work is a form of nurturing, and it changes how we feel about ourselves.

Much importance is made of physical fitness and personal training as forms of self-care. My Pilates teacher challenges me with weekly text messages, coaching me to show up. But there is also an internal, emotional kind of fitness that can be reached only through a nonphysical kind of self-care. This is the kind of training I coach.

When we have worked in our unexplored room, we hear a new voice altogether.

This is a voice that whispers, "You are enough."

When I first comprehended the truth of these words, my world turned upside down. "I am enough" was a theme my wife used when she taught fifth grade, but somehow I had missed this idea growing up. It is not what we normally learn from well-meaning, but conditional, human love.

"I am enough" is heart knowledge. It is the result of experience. It is the beginning of what we learn when we enter our unexplored room to do this work. It grows with certainty.

I first tasted this heart truth after a week of personal work in the mountains of Pennsylvania. On our last day, all the clients and therapists gathered in a circle, where we joined hands and sang along with Whitney Houston's recording: "The greatest love of all is happening to me. I found the greatest love of all, inside of me."

I was taught from an early age to have compassion *for others*. But I only began to find compassion for *myself* when I became vulnerable and my mask fell away. When I saw how everyone else was just like me, I saw myself in a softer light.

There was such beauty here, at the doorway of these stairs, leading downward.

Reflection

Find a quiet moment in a quiet place where you can be alone. If you can, sit comfortably with your feet on the floor and your back straight. Breathe in deeply. Breathe out deeply. Do this again until you notice your body relaxing.

As you feel relaxed, allow yourself to float above your thoughts and feelings. Notice any thoughts or feelings that emerge and let them go.

Take particular notice of your heart space.
Without thinking or conceptualizing, allow your heart speak to you.
What wounds come up for you?
What would it be like to look at yourself with a softer lens?

Test the words:
I own my power...

I deserve this...

I am enough...

Notice if any feelings come up with these messages.

Is your heart asking you to get smaller?

Or is your heart nudging you to expand?

You are not alone.
We all have loss, illness, and disappointment.
We all have an unexplored room
that contains a sense of unworthiness.

Imagine, for a moment, a warmth in your chest.
    Let the warmth grow.
Allow this warmth in your chest to create a sense of light.

Your heart space is actually a place of warmth and light.

Breathe in deeply, and then exhale fully. When you are ready, you can open your eyes.
Come back to the room where you are sitting.

Chapter Four
Enter the Wound

Digging in the dirt
Stay with me I need support
I'm digging in the dirt
Find the places I got hurt
Open up the places I got hurt

—Peter Gabriel

Surgeons have an uncomfortable expression about healing. They say that in order to cure a festering infection in the body, they have to "enter the wound." They have to open the abscess and drain it. It doesn't matter if the wound looks as if it is healed and is closed on the outside. It's kind of icky, but if there is a chronic infection in the body tissues underneath the skin, the only way to heal the patient is to "enter the wound."

There is a similar Buddhist tradition. The way to heal illness is to go inside it. If you have a headache, then it is your task to go inside the discomfort and sit with it. Ask the pain what it wants from you. Be with it. Some healing is possible only when we go inside the wound.

This is not something we like to think about much in our culture. But I think Peter Gabriel understood this when he wrote, "Digging in the dirt, to find the places I got hurt."

If we dig in the dirt, then we get dirt under our fingernails. It can get a little messy.

But what if there is something precious to be found here in the dirt? What if digging is the only way for us to find it?

This book differs from some kinds of self-help ones, because it is about action. Insight is good, but if you want to survive, action trumps insight. If you are thrown into a river, your knowledge of swimming will not save your life. Kicking your legs will. This book was written to inspire you to jump into the middle of the river and swim. Action is the only way we are able to move from one place to another.

I spent about ten years of my life relapsing from drug addiction and alcoholism. Even when I was attending AA meetings, I managed to stay clean and sober for only a year or two each time. I was stuck. I could not move forward with my recovery. When I was about thirty-five years old and clean again, I was desperate. This is when my beloved sponsor, Don M., suggested a different course of action. I sensed that he was right.

Don told me I needed to attend a workshop called the Family Program, which a nonprofit rehabilitation facility offered in the mountains of Pennsylvania.

Once, during a previous attempt at sobriety, I had been about nine months clean and sober when my girlfriend told me she was pregnant. By her previous boyfriend. While she was with me. I relapsed. Not long afterward, I was back at a men's AA meeting, trying to pick up the pieces of my life again and trying to understand what had just happened to me. The topic at the AA table was "relapse." As the circle went around, some old guy at the end of the table finally said, "Every single time that I have relapsed, right before I go back out, I have always said the same thing to myself: 'fuck it!'" He paused. "I eventually learned that relapsing was not my real enemy. 'Fuck it' was my enemy. If I wanted to stay sober, I had to avoid 'fuck it.'"

His words resonated with me. "Fuck it" was another phrase for despair. Despair was my real enemy, and it was an old, familiar visitor. I recalled how I'd felt after my girlfriend dumped me. Nothing had mattered anymore.

"What's the use?" I thought.

And then I relapsed.

Looking back, I now know the despair that kept disrupting my life came from my unexplored room. There are many causes of despair, but mine was the despair of abandonment. If I really wanted to learn how to stay clean and sober, I had to understand my abandonment wound.

The Family Program that my sponsor recommended to me was an experiential week-long program held in an old mansion. I had been in therapy many times over the years, but this program was something completely different. When I got there, I found myself mixing with a dozen other clients, and most were adults who had grown up in alcoholic homes. As the week unfolded, I quickly learned that most of my fellow clients had also been sexually molested in childhood. Neither family alcoholism nor molestation had happened to me.

So what was I even doing there?

It didn't take me long to find out.

Our first exercise on Sunday night was to dramatize, in a performance sculpture (with other clients), our family structure. When it was my turn, one man stood behind me to represent my dad. A woman hovered over me to represent my mom. I was asked to choose what role I had played in our family system. This was actually quite a profound question.

Had I been a mascot child, who had overachieved, made straight A's, and been captain of the football team?
No, not really.

Had I been a scapegoat child, who was acting out the family drama in public and getting in trouble?
Well, not really. At least not much.

I walked around the people playing my parents and found myself sitting behind them in the corner of the room. I was hiding. As I sat there with my stuffed animal, I felt waves of grief wash over me. I had found my role in our family system.
I had been a lost child.

When I was growing up, I learned to escape from our (nonalcoholic) family drama by any means possible, and my escape was often made through reading books and listening to records. I played by myself for hours every day as an only child, and I learned how to hide from family dysfunction at a very young age. When I sat on the floor with a stuffed animal and saw myself as a lost child, my tears welled up.

I acknowledged a wound.

This is when I realized something else. I really *did* belong here in this workshop.

Hello, unexplored room.

My dear parents adopted me when I was nine months old. I was their only son. I had always been told I was adopted, and my parents told me they loved me from the first day they saw me. My parents actually met my biological mother before the adoption, and they assured her they would be loving parents and would make sure I was educated.

I was walking on my friend's estate not long ago, admiring his work. He had built a free-standing sauna, a solar-powered outhouse, a free-standing work studio, and a wooden bridge that led to an outdoor labyrinth. It was a tour de force in resourcefulness. I asked him how he learned to do all this creative construction. He replied that his father and grandfather in rural Iowa had taught him that building was a form of self-reliance. For my friend, building had become a form of self-care. I was touched and impressed.

I found myself reflecting with him that I had grown up in a college apartment in a men's residence hall, where my dad was a dean. There was never any yard work, and there was never anything to fix. I found myself noticing I had learned something different from my dad: how to connect with my heart.

My dad spent his entire life counseling young men in college. He was beloved by many, and he certainly loved his work. He was a human being with many faults, but in his better moments, I think he was able to sense the emotional energy of his students. He was also able to connect with me. We had our struggles, but it is my certainty that when I was first adopted, what I found in his eyes was love.

As the years progressed, my dad became overwhelmed with his work and was less available to us. My mom responded by becoming overinvolved. She became her own worst critic (and mine) and worked intensely to be the perfect parent. It would have destroyed her to think she had made a mistake. This was true of my dad too. The most important part of their story line was this: "We have given Greg everything he ever needed."

Except for one thing.
They had no idea how to help me to acknowledge the wounds that commonly occur around adoption.

In adulthood, I later learned that my biological mother, Bette, had two other children. I have managed to spend some time with my older brother, Fred, who remembered when I was born. When I was a baby in the home, I was known as "Frankie." After I was adopted out, he remembered asking our mom, "Whatever happened to Frankie?"

Bluntly, it seemed to me that Frankie was voted off the island. When he was nine months old.

I am so grateful to my older brother, because he has provided me with a lot of factual information from this preverbal period in my life. He gave me pictures of my biological mother, who died in her fifties. I learned that she was a bright journalist with an English degree and that she also suffered from alcoholism. When she was married with two children, she had an affair at work, and I came along in a scandalous way in 1957. Her marriage fell apart. My biological father was well-known and married, with kids of his own. He provided Bette with exit money to leave Los Angeles.

Bette left California for Washington, DC, with me and my two siblings. We lived together until she learned she might be able to reunite with her husband, if I wasn't in the picture. I was an uncomfortable reminder of her affair. If she could find a new home for me, it might be the best choice for everyone. Even me.

Bette evaluated several couples and finally chose my adoptive parents. This generous, kind couple would take care of Frankie.

When I first met my biological brother and learned about the early parts of my own story, I was in my twenties. When I read my adoption records, I never experienced any emotion—it was only data to me. I had always been taught I had been given everything I needed, and I had completely internalized this message.
I reasoned, "If I had been given everything I needed, then how could I possibly be wounded?"

Being "not-wounded" is a mask we all are attached to, at first. We all want to think of ourselves as OK. But what if all of us have some kind of wound underneath everything? What if being wounded is a normal part of being human?

And what if our old wounds are what keep us stuck?

There is an uncomfortable truth here. If we are ever stuck in life, then it is probably because we have been wounded somewhere in our past.

To be human is to be wounded.

Author John Bradshaw has done some wonderful work in this area. According to Bradshaw, the wounds that affect us most often occur during various levels of development in childhood. Sometimes an injury even occurs in a preverbal period, as it did with me. When this happens, it is tougher to bring up any actual memories or mental pictures tied to the injury.

Bradshaw produced a marvelous series of audio meditations for different developmental phases of childhood, in order to help the listener regress back from adolescence to the toddler phase and even to infancy. As I listened to all his recordings, I tried to pay attention to which phase of childhood evoked the most intense feelings. It was during the infancy meditation that I felt the most grief. The time frame of my wound was unmistakable.

I think there are many other ways for us to recognize our hidden wounds. Another good way is for us to ask what stories touch us the most. What songs, movies, or books bring up the most sadness for us? The important thing is just to sit behind ourselves with curiosity. We must pay attention like a little bird, sitting on our own shoulder. We notice what kinds of feelings come up as the story plays. If we are able to sit in the dim light of our unexplored room, there will be something surprising for us to learn.

My core issue became the clearest for me on the third day of "pain camp" (as I affectionately renamed the family program). Each of us had worked in the unexplored room by writing letters to our parents, and we had allowed the unvented feelings of rage, sorrow, and despair to surface. We had all ventured into the personal peril of our childhood stories, because the therapists and clients alike had created an envelope of safety. A group culture had been established, and we had a shared purpose: We were there to heal. We were all willing to enter the wound.

For example, in our small work group, one member worked with a dead loved one. As one of us lay on the floor, he was able to talk to his estranged, dead father. There were many tears. Eventually, it was my turn. There was a young attorney in our group, who had a kind energy that I loved, and I asked her to play my biological mother, Bette. Bette stood next to me, looking down, holding a drink in her hands.
She was detached from me.

I allowed all the feelings to come up that I had repressed for my entire life.
I felt anger. I felt unbelievable despair.
I had waited all my life to meet her.
I cried.
I shouted at her, "You left me in a house of strangers!"
And then, a cry erupted from me that was long and high-pitched.
It was the cry of a little boy. It was a little broken-hearted cry.

This was a profound and holy moment in my life. At the age of thirty-five, my heart opened up for the first time, because I finally allowed myself to feel the emotional content of my own story.

The emotional circulation to my heart returned. I had named my despair. I allowed myself to reexperience the overwhelming emotion that kept welling up from my basement. This was the wound I had been living with. This was the pain I had attempted to medicate away. The light to my unexplored room had been turned on.

Abandonment was the core wound I entered that day. I needed to do more than admit the existence of the injury. To reconnect my heart with a story that was in my head, I had to go inside the wound and feel it again, as the little boy who was abandoned. I had to enter the wound. This was the crucial step for the healing that was ahead.

It finally became clear to me that childhood despair was what I had been attempting to medicate away. Every time I perceived any hint of abandonment, it turned into despair. When I first allowed my stored grief to surface in the mountains of Pennsylvania, my heart finally found a pathway to my head.

This new connection between my head and heart created desires that were life-changing for me. Once I had felt the pain of little Greg, I found a desire to protect him. This was the birth of self-care for me, and I began to attend support groups with others who had done family-of-origin work. I made conscious choices to nurture myself.

Sometimes, when we hear stories of other people's work, we feel a vague recognition that we also might store away pain somewhere in our lives. This is a recognition originating from a place we cannot see.

I probably first heard about this place when I studied Carl Jung in college; he's the one who named it "the shadow." Jung held that shadow is the part of our self that we are unconscious of. Like a shadow, it is shaped like us and stands right behind us, where we cannot see it. We are normally blind to our shadow, but it is walking with us anyway. Jung taught that shadow affects our words and actions in ways that can be quite curious. Sometimes shadow surfaces at work, and it often shows itself in our domestic partners or in our children. Our shadow can be obvious to others, even when we can't see it.

The term *shadow* implies a kind of darkness, as if it is a thing that is dangerous, something to be afraid of. This comes out when someone admits that they "struggle with their personal demons." If we imagine our shadow as something fierce, foreign, and menacing, then it is much more difficult to be with.

Imagining shadow as an unexplored room has been helpful to me. Rather than something dark and forbidding, or some kind of demon we should fear, the shadow becomes an ordinary place that is found inside all of us. And it is a place anyone can explore.

Exploration is action. It is a kind of work that requires more than reading. If we really want to get a sense of what is in our own unexplored room, we need someone else who can help us notice things we have been unconscious of. In addition to traditional talk therapy, exploration is found in experiences that have been designed to help us access our own unconscious material. These experiential programs are not about PowerPoint lectures and note-taking. They contain drama, music, art, and also creative, interactive exercises. Examples of such programs are given throughout this book.

There are many other ways to reconnect our emotional circulation. Sometimes, as in my experience, healing involves grief work. Sometimes it involves anger work or work with fear in a symbolic space. Everyone's work looks a little different.

Years ago, Suzi worked with her therapist on childhood sexual abuse. Her work led her to write a certified letter to the middle-school teacher who had molested her. The letter demanded that he give up working with children and enter therapy.

There are many names for the personal work that transforms our life space, but it usually involves entering our old wounds. Suzi's work with her shadow led her to speak up from a new sense of personal power.

Sometimes work in the unexplored room involves a kind of listening. It may involve hearing powerful affirmations of something we have always longed to hear. Sometimes work with the shadow involves recognizing and setting boundaries with those who are close to us. When we are ready to do this kind of work, our deeper self will call to us. What we need most will surface.

The work I have done is not unlike the kind of work my patients face, if serious illness comes to visit. When I see patients in my office regarding a mass in their lung, it is as if there are two diseases present. Yes, there is the lung mass, but there is also something else: the fear of the lung mass. We ask, "Could it be cancer?"

Fear is like a second disease and creates a great deal of havoc in our lives. Have you ever felt anxiety as you have waited for the results of a medical test? I have.

Greg Loewen

In addition to fear, serious illnesses can also bring up anger, depression, and even despair. And it is not only illness that does this; any kind of loss or grief can bring up the same emotions. Any kind of serious life event comes with emotional content. It may be a divorce. It may be the loss of a spouse or a child. It may be the loss of a job. Any of these may set the stage for doing work in our heart space when we are ready. Sometimes tragedy can create meaning in a good way.

I have now reached a point in my life where I no longer feel regret about being adopted. I am profoundly grateful for my parents and their love. I am also grateful for Bette and her love. In my better moments, I have even been grateful for my wound of abandonment and all I have learned from it. Abandonment itself has created my greatest strengths.

My sense of abandonment left me with an unintentional skill. Abandoned kids don't want to get abandoned again, so it is necessary for us to learn to read people in a sensitive way. This is because we need to know if we are in danger of being left again. This tendency for vigilance is often seen in children like me with attachment issues. As I grew up, I think my wound led me to see others in a sensitive way. In some ways, I think my abandonment is what taught me to read people and what they are feeling. This very skill became the backbone of my professional life and has helped me everywhere else too. My deepest wound has become my greatest strength.

Entering this space and admitting to the existence of a core wound was a turning point in my life. It was the beginning of my healing work. When I experienced the anger, despair, and grief of that moment, I was affirmed.

64

It wasn't my imagination!
I really *had* been hurt!
I finally gained a grip on my emotional life, and I have remained in recovery ever since.

I never met my biological mother physically, and she has been dead for many years. But throughout my life, the feeling that she let me go replayed like an old tape, whenever something hurtful happened to me. I finally met my biological mother in symbolic space, and I was given the chance to say what my inner child needed to say. When my child spoke, I gained access to this gentle, vulnerable part of myself.
I became more whole. This is the power of experiential work.

Our unexplored rooms contain many old wounds that can be entered and healed. This is work you can do too.
If we do not visit our past, then it will come to visit us.

Reflection

Create a quiet moment in a quiet place. Sit comfortably with your feet on the floor and your back straight, if you can. Breathe in deeply, and then exhale fully. Do this again. Notice your body beginning to relax.

In this relaxed space, say hello to any emotions that surfaced while you read this chapter.

Is there a part of my story that triggered something for you?
What pictures of your own childhood came up when you read this chapter?
Have you ever noticed how a rough spot in your life seems to resemble a way you were hurt long ago?

Have you ever sat with this wound?

To be human is to be wounded.

Can you imagine a bright light shining from inside this place?

Could there be a phenomenal gift that rests within your wound?

What will it cost you to enter here?

Breathe in deeply, and then breathe out deeply. Say hello to the fear.
Breathe in deeply, and then breathe out deeply. Say hello to the resistance.
Breathe in deeply, and then breathe out deeply. Say hello to the courage.

Breathe in deeply, and then exhale fully.

Open your eyes when you are ready to come back to the room where you are sitting.

Chapter Five

The Visitor

Tremble for yourself, my man,
You know that you have seen this all before

—Marcus Mumford

In my men's group, I was once given an affectionate nickname: Tank Commander. When I bought my new laptop a few years ago, I discovered a computer game called "Battle Supremacy." It was a World War II game where the player fights for survival against enemy tanks. When I first found it, I could play it for hours.

Each player has the opportunity to pick out a tank that suits his or her fighting style. I tended to pick tanks with powerful guns. The trade-off is that tanks with powerful guns are heavier, so they move more slowly and more awkwardly than others. To partially compensate for this, the armor on this kind of tank is distributed primarily in the front. Having the heaviest armor in the front makes my favorite tank extremely vulnerable to rear attacks.

In the middle of a tank battle with Internet opponents, an enemy tank often would sneak up behind me. When this happened, I would attempt to swing around to face my foe, but I was always too slow. The enemy would come up behind me and shoot me in the butt multiple times. I was dead. Dead and pissed off. When I was shot like this, I would even feel rage come up. Alone in the basement, I found myself screaming at the enemy tank and swearing at the computer screen. I wanted to restart the game and execute my revenge.

I am a reasonably peaceful guy, and I hate arguments and conflict. I imagine myself as an aging hippie sometimes. I have never served in the military, and I have never studied the martial arts. I have deep respect for those who have. I do not own any weapons. I tend to like gun control, and I have protested against wars. I even take modest pride in the peacemaking skills I draw upon at my work from time to time. It was embarrassing to me that I loved the tank game. And surprising.

I had to honestly ask myself why I was so drawn to this game.

When I sat with this question, I began to see that I was really hosting a shadowy visitor from my unexplored room. I decided to call my visitor Tank Commander, or TC. TC was a part of my unseen self that came out when I was playing the game. Sometimes, this is how our unexplored room comes upstairs to find us.

In order to understand this concealed part of myself, I had to, first and foremost, avoid being harsh with myself for loving to play this silly game. I had to welcome TC with some neutrality and curiosity. Next, I tried to imagine a conversation with this alienated part of me, sitting before me in an empty chair. I asked the empty chair that held TC's energy, "What have you come to teach me?"

When I sat in the chair, the answer that surfaced was a bit surprising. TC replied that he loved to fight. He loved beating an opponent, even more than he loved the strategy of reading the battle. TC was about my own basic instincts. If I am under a threat, then apparently, there is a part of me that loves the fight.

This was certainly something new for me to admit. But there seemed like there might be more about anger. I asked TC, "Is this where my rage really comes from?"

TC also had something to teach me about rage. He pointed out that what triggered me the most was an attack from the rear!

As I worked on this in my men's group, I learned that there really was a part of me that hated to be attacked, if I had failed to defend myself. As I sat with this, I could see that underneath my own anger was a kind of humiliation that I had failed to protect myself. When I fail to cover my own flank and am caught, I feel ashamed.

From looking at my reaction to a video game, I started to own the fact that I did not defend myself well in many other situations. When I looked at my life, I could remember times when I was attacked from the rear, because I had allowed it to happen. I once allowed an office manager to dictate to me how I ran my own office. I went home feeling very angry for weeks, when this happened. I had failed to protect my flank.

I could see that I needed to learn how to defend my own boundaries better, as a competent warrior. Here was a visitor from my unexplored room, showing me where my work was. As I talked about this in my men's group with other men, my boundaries became stronger. My visitor became integrated into my life.

Our sense of identity is usually tied to what we do (our career), who we are with (our partner), or what we love (our pastimes). This is when a behavior shows a hidden part of ourselves that we have been blind to. Perhaps we blow up at something trivial. Perhaps we catch ourselves doing something unthinkable or completely out of character. We are not who we imagined ourselves to be, and it can be scary. This is what it looks like when a visitor from our unexplored room comes upstairs. One way of recognizing that our unexplored room has been visited is to ask ourselves questions like these:

- Have I ever had negative emotions that were out of proportion to whatever happened?
- Do I ever find myself doing the very thing I have hated in someone else?
- Is there an embarrassing secret habit in my life that I have difficulty giving up?

Whenever a strong emotion is present (e.g., fear, sadness, or anger), the emotion is often about something other than what is happening in the present moment. Our most intense feelings often have a larger meaning that usually comes from underneath. If, when they pass, we can reflect on them, the strong feelings also can tell us something about what our expectations of the world should be. These worldviews were formed as we grew up but lie unchallenged until a crisis occurs.

The unexplored room is another way of describing the human shadow. Robert Bly points out that our shadows are almost invisible at noon, but they grow longer during the day. At night, there is nothing left of us but shadow. In a poetic way, in the daytime, we exhibit only the parts of ourselves that we are comfortable with. At high noon, our shadow is concealed from those who are around us, and from ourselves. But as the day goes on, our shadow looms behind us. Even though we cannot see it, our friends and family can.

At night, Bly points out that the shadow becomes very long, and when we sleep, the shadow is all that is left of us. In a sense, we become shadow completely in our dreams. During sleep, we may dream that our father is a monster, even though in the daytime we insist, "My dad was wonderful to me." Our shadow knows that this line is not completely true, and it compensates for this tension by creating an unrecognizable dream version of our father. The truth is probably somewhere in between. Yes, Dad was wonderful sometimes, and sometimes he could be like a monster. Dreams are a wonderful place for us to glimpse our shadow material and are another way our unexplored room comes to visit us.

Another way to describe the unexplored room is that it is a bag we carry behind us. In another of Bly's word pictures, all our emotions are acceptable when we are infants. But as we grow up, we begin to learn that some emotions, such as rage or anger, are not acceptable to our parents. If this is true, then rage goes in the bag.

Perhaps joy or silliness is not acceptable in our home. If this is so, then our humor goes into the bag, and we go through life with a stiff, sober outlook. Perhaps grief or sorrow is not acceptable, if we are told not to cry when we are little. If this is so, then grief and sorrow go into the bag, and we find it difficult to cry as adults.

We may learn that sexuality is not acceptable. Then sex also goes into the bag. We may learn that creativity should not be expressed, if we are told, "Play the music on the page," or "Only color between the lines."

When this happens, then creativity may go into the bag.

We may learn that our voice is not acceptable. Asking for what we want or need may go into the bag. The things we put into the bag are not always happy there.

During the second half of life, we begin to remember the contents of our bag. Creativity knocks on our door, and we feel a new hunger to sing, dance, or write. We want our creativity back. We may find our sexuality visiting us with an affair, or with erotica and masturbation, if we want our sexuality back. We may find ourselves speaking up unexpectedly if we want our voice back.

Everything we tried to repress in our bag will eventually visit us.

On the other hand, we don't have to wait for visitors. We can make a decision to look into the bag and reclaim what we have repressed. This kind of activity has been called, among other things, shadow work. Shadow work is just another way to describe working on our stuff. It is something we all can do when we are ready.

Sometimes doing this kind of work is prompted by emotional triggers in our lives. Trauma creates pathways of stress within our central nervous system that persist for years after the event is over. For example, if we have been wounded in a particular way in our childhood, any similar event in adulthood may easily activate this pathway. When this happens, it triggers the same emotions that first happened when we were wounded.

My wife and I struggled with sexuality when we were first married. Suzi carried with her some traumatic pathways from her childhood sexual abuse. When we were intimate, there were times my touch would trigger old abuse memories for her. She would stiffen, shake, and then shut down. Our sexuality would have to be postponed. I really struggled with this back then. There were times when I would roll over onto my side of the bed, overcome with complete despair.

We eventually entered couple's therapy with a kind, insightful psychiatrist and his wife. In one of our first sessions, our therapist gently pointed out something shocking to me: Suzi was not the only one with an emotional trigger in the bedroom.
I was also being emotionally triggered.

Hello, unexplored room.

As I began to greet my own emotional triggers, I had to admit that perhaps the despair I wrestled with was not new. And it was not really about my wife, who clearly loved me. My despair and deep sadness were about something deeper. When sexual closeness was impossible for my wife, I felt that old, familiar despair of abandonment again.

When I was triggered in the bedroom, my intense emotions had little to do with the present moment. My feelings instead were only an echo from traumatic pathways created over fifty years ago. My emotional trigger was my unexpected visitor.

I began to work with this new visitor over the years and created a new practice of self-care in my life. As I did my own self-care, I found that my emotional triggers around our struggle as a couple began to disappear.

It is not uncommon for us to find visitors from our unexplored room when we are engaged in long-term relationships. We may find ourselves noticing that our spouse or partner is doing the exact same thing our mother or father did. Our visitor may resemble someone who is well-known to us.

Sometimes our unexplored room will visit us in the form of something we despise. Remember the story of the fundamentalist preacher who made his career out of denouncing gays, only to be caught with a gay prostitute? Hello again to the unexplored room. If there is someone we really hate, the chances are high that he is really someone who inhabits our own space in an unseen way.

In the movie *Patton*, George C. Scott enters the hospital tent in Sicily and talks to wounded soldiers to encourage and honor them. But as he is leaving the tent, he sees a soldier who is weeping. He asks the soldier what is wrong, and the soldier replies that he was unable to tolerate the guns and the shelling any longer.

In the movie, Patton is enraged, strikes him with his gloves, and calls the man a "yellow-bellied coward." He tells the shaking, crying soldier he is sending him back to the front, where he may be shot. Patton's rage grows as he speaks. He demands the man be removed from the hospital tent. As Patton moves to draw his pistol, the doctors and orderlies quickly pull the man from Patton's view.

I found myself looking at Patton harshly for his abusive rage when I first rewatched the movie to write this chapter. But of course, whenever we judge someone, it is time to take a look inward. I had to admit that this chapter started with my own rage and abusive energy, which came up when I played a computer game. What do I find now, if I look in my own unexplored room? General Patton.

Patton's trigger was a weeping, broken soldier. Here was the grief and brokenness he could not allow himself to feel. Here was a soldier who also had faced war and who was overwhelmed with emotions on his hospital cot. Patton seemed to come unglued with a very human rage, triggered by the very same wounds of war. This is because grief and brokenness can climb up from our unexplored room to trigger rage.

It is possible that Patton might not have reacted in that moment if he'd had access to a kind of care all soldiers deserve. Historians speculate that if Patton could have maintained mastery of himself in the historical moment depicted in the movie, he would not have lost the command of the seventh army.

It is said that in order to be effective in battle, warriors must gain mastery over their anger and fear. It is even possible for us to be afraid of our own fear. If this is so, then the fear we hate in others is really our own fear. We are all alienated from our own fear at times. Whenever this happens, our emotions are just waiting to surface.

Some things are put into the unexplored room by our society or culture. Mental illness has been put there. From World War I to recent times, mental illness (including PTSD) was not an illness to the military. Patton was not the only one in denial. Karl Marlantes observed, "The military has actually made improvements, so people are considering post-traumatic stress disorder as, at the least, a possible psychological problem. You know, when I was in Vietnam, it was just considered malingering."

Comedian George Carlin observed that, according to the military, "shell shock" later became "battle fatigue," which became "post-traumatic stress disorder." This was a way of verbally sanitizing trauma. Our struggle to accurately name this illness could also be viewed as a sign of growth. Eventually society decides to take out some of the things it has buried in everyone's unexplored room and name them.

In his brilliant book *What It Is Like to Go to War*, Vietnam veteran Karl Marlantes argues that counseling should be mandatory for all soldiers who return from active duty. More needs to be done. Creative arts programs like "Warrior Songs" offer veterans a kind of work in the shadow with art, music, and community, as a response to this gap in available service to veterans. Those with trauma in their past who want to do this work can find programs designed for trauma, although more programs are needed. In doing work like this, it is possible to allow our combustible material to surface in a safe environment, instead of permitting it to blow up our lives.

I wrote this chapter with the naïveté and respect of someone who has never experienced combat and who has never faced the burden veterans silently carry. But all of us hail visitors from our unexplored room. We can turn their arrival into healing, and it is a lot easier to do this work with some help. The unexplored room lies within the middle of our blind spot, where everything is difficult to see—even with a good book, a journal, and a pen.

Work with our visitors completely changes when we gain an outside point of view. This kind of help can come from a community of others who have also done their work, as it did with my men's group. It could also come from a skilled therapist (who has had to do his or her own work too). It is much easier for others to help us process our shadow material if they have already processed some of their own.

Our visitors from below are powerful teachers when we are ready to listen.

Reflection

Create a quiet moment where you can be alone. Sit comfortably with your feet on the floor and your back straight, if you can. Breathe in deeply. Breathe out deeply. Do this again until you notice your body beginning to relax.

As you relax, notice any feelings that have surfaced for you while reading this chapter. Allow anything to surface that wants to…

Can you remember a moment when you found yourself doing something surprising?
When have you found yourself overreacting to something in an unexpected way?
What situations or people really light you up?
Have you ever noticed when your spouse or partner does something that makes you feel like you are a child again?
Is this a visitor from your unexplored room?
Can you, with gentle neutrality, say hello to these parts of you?
Does your deeper self want to understand your visitor?

Breathe in deeply, and then exhale fully. Open your eyes when you are ready to come back to the room where you are sitting.

Chapter Six

Treasure

There's a light in the depths of your darkness
There's a calm at the eye of every storm
There's a light in the depths of your darkness
Let it shine
Oh, let it shine.

—Dan Fogelberg

In the brilliant Ben Stiller film *The Secret Life of Walter Mitty*, we watch as the mythic Walter is seemingly lost in adventure fantasies as his boring job and boring love life slowly unravel. Walter works at *LIFE* magazine as a negative asset manager (a great play on words) and often seems spaced out. He is absent throughout his day, escaping into a vibrant fantasy life. Walter acts timid and fearful and avoids all risks. He is in love with a coworker, but he can't even talk to her. Walter doesn't know it, but he is disconnected from his own heart.

Walter wasn't always like this. In a scene in Central Park, we are surprised to see Walter demonstrate a few dazzling skateboard tricks to a boy; in another scene, Walter's mother finds a picture of teen-age Walter, sporting a Mohawk haircut crafted by his father. We learn that the uptight, conservative, and fearful Walter was once a skateboard punk poised to explore Europe and the rest of the world.

Then, when Walter was seventeen, his father died. There were no savings. We learn that when this happened, Walter went out, got a haircut, and found a job in a fast-food restaurant. When Walter's father died, something big had to be stored in Walter's hidden space. He forgot about this part of himself for many years. Buried in the unexplored room were his courage and sense of adventure.

Walter's mother gives him an old box, which contains a time cap-sule Walter created when he was seventeen. The box holds an un-used European travel diary given to young Walter by his father, and he finds himself returning to study it. We watch as Walter reclaims courage and adventure from the time capsule.

He eventually flies to Greenland, Iceland, and the Himalayas. He rides in a helicopter with a drunk pilot, swims with sharks, and skateboards beneath a volcanic eruption. Walter reclaims his love of risk and a sense of adventure from the new territory within his own heart. He is transformed by the treasure he uncovered.

Jung taught that shadow material is not always dark. Sometimes the unconscious contains surprising brightness and richness. It is like finding an old master oil painting of priceless value, forgot-ten behind discarded boxes. Sometimes, the treasure buried in the unexplored room is called the "white shadow." It is the good stuff within our shadow.

An example of a white shadow might be seen in an aggressive, cutthroat CEO who does anything necessary to put his adversaries out of business. He buys their companies, dismantles them, and then sells them. In order to survive in a hostile childhood environment, he was taught that he must succeed at everyone else's expense. Sensitivity and generosity were buried in his unexplored room.

One day, the CEO goes through a midlife crisis that upends his life. Perhaps he loses a spouse or child or faces a serious illness. As he processes his loss, he realizes that winning at the expense of others has become empty. His entire life has become meaningless. As he looks inward, he discovers a surprising desire. He wants to give something back to the world. He leaves his predatory company and starts a nonprofit that helps the poor. He has discovered his white shadow.

I think our unconscious desires are what Joseph Campbell refers to as "our bliss." Campbell's central teaching was that we should follow our bliss. The first half of life is about achieving our goals, but in order for us to achieve them, our bliss must go into the basement. It is impossible for us to follow our bliss, if we are unconscious of the things that delight us. Recovery is needed. In order to follow our bliss, we have to recover it.

Many years ago, my mentor first challenged me to look inward, in order to help me recover my bliss. In our e-mails, his questions helped me begin to say hello to my white shadow.

He began by asking, "Who were your greatest teachers in life?"

I wrote back to him: "My greatest heroes were always teachers...my high-school biology teacher, my college organic chemistry teacher, and my med-school cardiology teacher. I wanted to be like them."

He asked, "If your life is a university degree, what is your curriculum? What are you here to learn?"

I replied, "I would have to say that it seems like I am here to learn something about relationships and something about healing."

"What stories and characters do you most resonate with?"

I answered, "My first choice is the fictional character Atticus Finch in Harper Lee's novel *To Kill a Mockingbird*." Atticus was a man with eloquence, dignity, and courage. He resisted hatred with calm understanding.

But the most important question that lay underneath his queries was this: What do these characters possess that seems to be missing in your life?

Atticus was part of my white shadow. As I sat with this question, I became conscious of something surprising. I certainly did not identify with the fearful and ignorant men who opposed Atticus. But Atticus did have something I found to be elusive in my own life. Dignity. I began to see what I might be missing.

Like my dad, my sense of humor had always been about self-deprecation. We both had a habit of making fun of ourselves in order to make people laugh. You could say our family had a tradition to keep dignity buried away in the basement. But I loved the way Atticus carried himself with dignity. I loved the way he treated everyone with dignity. He inspired dignity in others. I longed for something that was buried in my own unexplored room.

It is now time for me to admit something many men would find to be a little embarrassing. One of my other movie heroes is a ten-year-old girl with pigtails. Her name is Pollyanna.

I first saw the Disney movie when I was ten years old and loved it. I was in my fifties when I most recently watched it, and I have to be honest: I still found myself in tears through the story. If we freely allow our emotions to come up and pay attention to them, they can reveal some remarkable things.

The term *Pollyanna* has become a derogatory label for a person in the la-la land of idealized denial. But this is an unfair description of the character depicted in this movie.

Pollyanna was authentic. She did not project great power, but she seemed unconscious of power gradients. As a young girl, she was unintimidated by the middle-aged, fiery reverend Karl Malden. She challenged him to pick "glad texts" out of the Bible. Malden was one who thundered at his congregation, "Death comes unexpectedly!" To him, life was dangerous and abysmal. After Pollyanna came into his life, he had to rethink his take on hell and damnation.

Malden adopted her "glad texts" into his sermons at church. The world grew a little less perilous to him, and he became a warmer person.

Pollyanna also moves with equal authenticity through the life of the hypochondriacal Agnes Moorhead character, who is obsessed with her own death. Moorhead feigns illness in bed, picking out caskets with the funeral home director. Pollyanna is unafraid of Moorhead's anger and hangs crystals in her bedroom window. She creates homemade rainbows for her. Moorhead reengages with life and discovers beauty all around her. She eventually sells crystals and quilts for the town charity bazaar and becomes an enthusiastic fund-raiser.

Again, this key question resurfaced: What do Atticus and Pollyanna possess that seems to be missing in your life?

My truth was that, in some ways, I was a lot like Malden and Moorhead. I was a guy who struggled with a fearful view of the world, and I secretly believed that death does come unexpectedly. I was also someone who repeated secret negative self-talk and told myself, "You can never do that!"

As I sat with Pollyanna, I began to see why I longed for her authenticity. Her power was grounded in spiritual optimism. I grew up with a mom who worried about everything and believed something bad was just about to happen to us. In our family culture, my personal power was buried in the cellar.

As I did the exercise, I became conscious of how I loved dignity and authentic power. These were the key elements of my own white shadow.

Atticus and Pollyanna are more than characters from a story—they are archetypes.

Greg Loewen

Archetype is the word for a person who symbolizes a kind of energy found in human experience. Exploring an archetype is one way of touching our white shadow. If there is a particular character in a story that really means something to us, it is because there is resonance between the character and the part of ourselves we cannot see. Archetypes lead us to treasure concealed in our unexplored room.

George Lucas understood this well when he created *Star Wars*. Lucas acknowledges that the character Luke Skywalker would not exist if he had not read *The Hero with a Thousand Faces* by Joseph Campbell. Luke's story is a new version of the ancient, universal myth Joseph Campbell named the "Hero's Journey." The Hero's Journey is repeated in the arts through every era, from Homer's Odysseus to *Finding Nemo*.

When I was thinking about this chapter, I rewatched the first *Star Wars* trilogy, which I have always loved. The first episode came out during my first year in medical school, and I stood in a line in Kansas City that went around the block to see the movie. Like countless others, I resonated with the lead character, Luke Skywalker. One key element of Luke's journey as a hero was his struggle with his father.

Darth Vader is Luke's archenemy throughout the entire epic. In *The Return of the Jedi*, after Luke learns that Darth Vader is actually his father, the two engage in hand-to-hand combat in a battle for life and death. Eventually, Vader lies dying on the floor. He removes his helmet to look at Luke, and they hold each other in Vader's final moments. In this mythic scenario, son and father see each other eye to eye. They connect with each other.

Like Luke, I experienced a struggle with my larger-than-life dad. Towering over me at six foot seven, he was a gentle giant to many of us. As I grew older and began to see his darker human side too, there were moments when he seemed a little more like Darth to me. Looking back, I can now recognize my own life within Luke's story.

I spent my early years rebelling against the things my father loved. My dad had a singsong way of preaching to me and others, and I felt that he dominated our family with prayers and righteous posturing. He also kept a few secrets that I knew well. He could not be open with me about what he really struggled with. Like Darth, his helmet was on. I was repelled by his posturing and stung by what felt like phoniness. But at the same time, I also loved his kindness and his connection with me.

In men's work, I learned that the negativity I projected onto my dad could be found within myself. I too loved to posture at the center of the stage. I too kept my own secrets. Like my dad, I also loved to dominate the crowd with my brand of "spirituality." And I loved to connect to and help others. In a complicated way, I was exactly like what I imagined him to be.

As I worked on how I felt about him in this archetypal story, I found myself again repeating the mantra of Ram Das: "I am that too."

At the end of the movie, Luke wanted (on some level) to save his dying father. Perhaps on a deeper level, Luke really wanted to save himself. I could see how I reenacted this chapter of the *Star Wars* myth during the last months of my own dad's life, when his helmet came off a little. Dad and I connected in a deeper way than we ever had before, and within that connection, I saw even more of myself in him. I found treasure.

I have a friend who jokingly tells me that "men's work" means fixing the toilet and "women's work" means making supper for the kids. But there is another kind of men's work found within the unexplored room. This is a work where we look at our stuff, and we do so with other men. This is what changes our lives (and it also alters what tasks we imagine that men or women should do).

The men's movement over the past four decades grew out of the consciousness that there was something important to be passed down, from seniors to those who are entering adulthood. This work of initiation was critiqued by sociologist Michael S. Kimmel, who wrote that "men's work" fails to teach men traditional feminine strengths such as nurturing and engagement. In my personal experience, nurturance and sensitivity are the key features of the men's work he dismisses. Men learn to nurture one another. Men learn to be sensitive with one another. To experience such care from men is the most powerful way to understand and work through the injuries we have all lived through as men.

In a parallel way, this is also true of women's work.

My own experience tells me that men's work has made me an easier man to live with, as a husband. Writer David Deida observes that one of the deepest feminine pleasures occurs "when a man stands full, present, and un-reactive in the midst of his woman's emotional storms. When he stays present with her, and loves her through the layers of wildness and closure, then she feels his trustability, and she can relax."

Suzi and I have experienced the truth of this idea in our own relationship. No one has been a greater fan of my "men's work" than she has.

Men's work uses archetypes to identify the unseen gold within ourselves. The four central archetypes described by Jung were expanded by writers Moore and Gillette in their classic work, *King, Warrior, Magician, Lover: Rediscovering the Archetypes of the Mature Masculine*. These are widely used in the tradition of "men's work."

Gillette and Moore observed that some men instinctively relate to the mythical figure of Magician. This is the figure who holds the qualities of reflection and introspection. A Magician knows more than he reveals. In some cultures, the concept of Magician is held by the totem animal of the bear.

Other men are drawn to the King archetype. The King holds the energy of kindness and power with fairness and authority. The King is sometimes represented by the totem of the snowy owl, which symbolizes the gray hair of the elders.

A third archetype that resonates with some is the Lover. The Lover holds connectedness and gentleness and is often represented by the songbird and its music.

Finally, the fourth archetype is the Warrior, who holds bravery in the face of danger and determination in the face of adversity. The Warrior is often represented by the totem animal of the loyal dog.

In their book, they teach that every man has aspects of all four archetypes; we need a mixture of all of these qualities to show up as mature, healthy men.

Many other archetypes are found within religious myths and the fairy tales of world literature. In women's work, the corresponding archetypes might include the Wise Woman, the Queen, the Lover, and—interestingly—the Mother. Imagine the ferocity of a mother bear that protects her cubs and her warrior-like energy is immediately apparent. Many other archetypes are found in women's studies, and Jean Shinoda Bolen and others have written eloquently on this topic.

Our modern Western society no longer requires rites or rituals to symbolize our initiation as mature men or women. The blossoming of men's work and women's work in recent decades opens us up to an opportunity for spiritual growth. In these gender-based experiences, we find something that is not found anywhere else. Men's work and women's work provide us access to treasure that is nearly impossible to uncover on our own.

Several years ago, I attended a men's retreat, and one of the exercises required us to sit in silence. We were asked to allow the image of an animal to surface that "wanted to identify with us." We were challenged to not merely think of which animals we had loved in the past. We were asked to step below our thoughts and allow any picture to come up. I was surprised to find what came up for me.

An African lion appeared in my mind with a golden mane and a roar. *Lion* seemed like the opposite of me. For much of my life, I had tried to be a man of the eighties. I had always tried to be gentle and sensitive, like so many Alden Alda characters on the screen. My ferocity was concealed deep in the basement, because I'd put it there on purpose. And it was not just my ferocity. This totem of Lion held grounded power that was calm and neutral to any emotional storm.

I grew up in my father's tall shadow as a kid. He was a dean at his university and a public figure in our community. As a boy, I felt as if there was no place in our family system for me to have my own sense of dominion. And yet, now a stately African lion with grounded power and sovereignty had surfaced in my consciousness. The archetype of Lion was to be my totem animal.

During this men's retreat, we were all challenged to do personal work and to talk about our personal struggles. I dove into the process with all my heart, as did everyone in our group—everyone except for one fellow. He was a thin anxious man who vacillated about why he was there at the men's weekend. First he said, "I came here for myself." Later, he claimed, "I actually came here for my friend."

The man kept insisting that his life was really OK. The staff members tried to engage with him, encouraging him to take a risk and to work on his life with the rest of us. The anxious man managed to create a lot of drama by being helpless and indifferent at the same time. To me, it seemed that the entire group process stalled because of his drama.

The leader of the weekend retreat was an older Australian man named Billy, who walked over to our group and interrupted us. With calm dignity and grounded power, he decreed, "Enough! You are done!"

Billy could see that the drama was really a payoff for the man, and he challenged the behavior and ended it right there. Our group immediately restarted our work. Just like that. Billie's powerful intervention moved and inspired me. I had never seen anything like it.

The anxious man who had created so much drama seemed a little hurt at first and cried, "Wait!" But it was over for him...sort of. Because of Billie's intervention, the helpless, anxious man reengaged, and he returned to work more deeply than anyone else over the rest of the weekend. He changed before our eyes.

All of this unfolded because Billy cut through the bullshit. To me, this was dignity. It was regal Lion behavior.

I later shared a meal with Billy after the weekend was over and told him how inspired I had felt during his intervention. This was so powerful to me. I told Billy, "I want to be like you someday."

Billy smiled back at me and replied, "Once you spot it, you got it." His little remark held the magic at the core of this chapter.

"Spotting it" is how we own the richness buried in our unexplored rooms.

This is what changed Walter Mitty: he spotted adventurous courage in others, and he spotted it within himself.

I thought about Billy's words to me.
Was there really authentic power and regal dignity within me?

In the last months of my dad's life, when our helmets came off, I told him a little bit about my men's weekend retreat. I found myself sharing with Dad that I had taken on the spirit (and the name) of "Lion" in my men's group at home.

Dad replied, "That's really good, Greg. That's what our last name, 'Loewen,' actually means in German: 'Lion.' You come from a tribe of lions."

From my dad, I learned that my own name means "Lion."
I come from a tribe of lions. I don't have to become a lion: I am one already.
I became conscious of something that was always there inside me.
When my awareness grew, those around me noticed that I had shifted.
My wife could see a change in me.
Like Walter Mitty, my presence shifted in my love life, at work, and in my community.

There is treasure in our unexplored rooms.
To find it, we must dig.
It is waiting for us.

Reflection

Create a quiet moment in a quiet place. Sit comfortably with your feet on the floor and your back straight, if you can. Breathe in deeply, and then exhale fully. Do this again until you notice your body beginning to relax.

Within your relaxation,
    once again, find your heart.
Allow yourself to touch into something you desire the most.
    Let even the forbidden desires for your life to bubble up.

What strength do you wish you could embody?
What attribute do you admire in others?
Is there a book character or movie character who you wish you could be?
Is there a quality that character has that you long to have?

The quality that you long for is already yours.
It is your treasure.

If you are reading this chapter and doing this reflection,
    then you have already found treasure.
        It is courage.

Touch into the courage within your own heart.

Affirm yourself.

Sit and breathe into your courage.

Breathe in deeply, and then breathe out deeply.
Open your eyes when you are ready to come back to the room where you are sitting.

Chapter Seven
To Make Love Stay

All you have to do is stay

—Taylor Swift

When I was in my twenties, the novel *Still Life with Woodpecker* was one of my favorite books. Author Tom Robbins begins his satirical story with a simple question: "How do you make love stay?" This became the elusive, central question in the early chapters in my own life.

John Gottman has studied hundreds of couples in his Seattle-based "love lab" over many decades and has made powerful observations about what seems to makes love go away. He has noticed, for instance, that one of the most powerful predictors of divorce is a seemingly innocent behavior: One spouse rolls his or her eyes while the other is talking. For example, if one spouse reports an upsetting behavior and is critical of her partner, and her partner rolls his eyes in response, the relationship is in deep trouble. Beneath that facial expression, according to Gottman, lies something toxic to sustained connection: rolling the eyes may mean contempt. Veiled sarcasm, mockery, or hostile humor can silently dissolve the connection between two people.

But when I think back to what might have dissolved my first love, I don't remember rolling my eyes. I don't remember thinking negatively, with sarcasm or mockery.
I was eighteen.

Suzi and I had been together for about a year, and we had become very close, despite pressure from my parents, who were uncomfortable with the level of intimacy we appeared to have. We loved each other. After we had been together for a year, Suzi began to share some of her deeper issues with me. She told me about her experience with previous sexual abuse. She described her loneliness and her feelings of emptiness. When I glimpsed her struggle with depression, I was overwhelmed.

I was overwhelmed, because at eighteen, she was admitting to things I had not yet learned to talk about. I could actually relate to her, in a scary way. I was nowhere near being ready to be this honest about my own emotional life. It would take me nearly another decade to become this open. I was afraid and found I didn't know what to do or say.

I didn't know how to set boundaries with my parents, who opposed our relationship, and I didn't know how to trust Suzi in this way. I did not know how to just be present with her struggle with depression. So I finally did something that became a pattern for many of my future relationships. When my feelings became uncomfortable, I shut down completely. I was afraid and didn't know what to do, so

Greg Loewen

I became a stone wall and ended our relationship. I refused to talk to her.

Thirty years later, we found each other again. When I was living in New York, she sent out a group e-mail for New Year's, and for the first time, I was on her list of recipients. I wrote five pages back to her instantly. I couldn't believe I might have a second chance with her, and I knew my love for her had never completely ended. She wrote back to me. We called each other. A month later, I traveled out west to see her. We cautiously restarted our relationship.

One day, many months later, I found myself looking at her bookshelf in Oregon and discovered a little children's book called *Hope for the Flowers* by Trina Paulus. Inside the front cover of Suzi's book was a surprising inscription: a note written to Greg, from Suzi. It was dated Christmas of 1975.

Suzi wrote to me that she loved this book so much she was giving it to me for Christmas. This had been her gift to me after we had broken up. I realized that, many years ago, this used to be my book! But when I had received it from Suzi back in 1975, my heart was closed. I vaguely remember being insulted when I received the gift of a children's book, and I had sent it back to her without even reading it. But now, embarrassingly, my book had returned. This book had patiently waited for me in my unexplored room for thirty years.

I sat down to read *Hope for the Flowers* for the first time. *Hope* is an illustrated children's story about two caterpillars named Yellow and Stripe. The caterpillars love each other, but Stripe decides to leave to climb to the top of a heap. The heap is made up of other caterpillars. Left alone, Yellow enters the darkness of her own cocoon, and then emerges from the cocoon as a beautiful yellow butterfly. Yellow, the butterfly, then flies back to find Stripe. He recognizes her, even though she has changed, and he knows he still loves her. Stripe is finally ready to leave his old life of climbing upward.

The book ends as Stripe himself enters his own cocoon and emerges as a striped butterfly. This deep little children's book started to feel like a prophecy to me. It seemed to predict what I was about to face. And the book also hinted that perhaps love would stay.

When Suzi and I started seeing each other in the present era, a lot of water had passed under the bridge. She was going through her first divorce, and I was going through my third. We were thousands of miles apart. In a sense, it was perfect. We had found a powerful connection with each other that we treasured, but we also found ourselves in a kind of space that permitted us to do personal work. I knew in my heart that if I did not work on my interior in a new way, it was highly likely I would have four divorces, instead of three. I was finally ready to work on how to make love stay.

When I first joined AA many years before, I had learned a new concept: In order to really stay sober, I had to work on my own stuff. In AA, it is often repeated that each of us has to "clean up our own side of the street." It doesn't matter how much garbage is strewn on the opposite side of the street, and it doesn't matter that someone else is in the wrong. We are responsible for what we have done. We are responsible for our side of the street.

So if we go to our AA sponsor, complain about our spouse, and complain about the awful things he or she has done, our sponsor will usually reply by asking us, "So what is your responsibility in the whole story? What is on your side of the street?"

The garbage on our side of the street is yet another metaphor for the reality of the unexplored room. The pathway of recovery tends to fail unless it winds through this dark space. Yes, there are old beliefs about ourselves that need to be discarded like garbage. Yes, there are the old roadmaps of life that our parents believed, which no longer work for us and must be released or redrawn as well. But there are many things to be found in the unexplored room.

When I wanted to start a new relationship with Suzi, I had to reflect on my past. I had managed to leave three marriages in a row. This speaks for itself. No matter what I imagined on my ex-wives' side of the street, there had to be some stuff for me to clean up over on my side. I resolved to work in earnest.

One of the ideas that caught my attention at that time was the concept of "attachment." The importance of attachment was recognized by John Bowlby and Mary Ainsworth, who showed that when a toddler was separated from familiar people, as happens in adoption, it could have long-term negative impacts on the child's emotional life. Attachment was a hot idea in the area of adopted kids. As I read about it, it seemed to me that attachment might be something I lacked in the realm of relationship.

Psychologist Arthur Becker-Weidman writes that attachment is "an enduring emotional tie between two people." Attachment is something that is "grounded in trust" and is "built upon a history of shared experiences." I read about how adopted and foster kids are separated from their primary caregiver and find it difficult or even impossible to attach to their adopted parents. Kids with attachment issues sometimes struggle to open their hearts, even to those who deeply love them. It began to dawn on me that my difficulty with attachment was this: love didn't stay because *I* did not stay.

I found an attachment disorders clinic and made an appointment. The waiting room was filled with toys, and the therapist told me she did not usually work with adults but was still willing to try to help me. After a few sessions together, she told me I actually did not have RAD, or "reactive attachment disorder." But she assured me I was still in the right place. I clearly had the attachment issues her clinic was created for.

Sometimes love is a feeling. This much is clear. Love may be a feeling that comes and goes. But when we are infants, we are completely unaware of how love is also a decision. Sometimes the attachment within love is found inside a decision to get up in the night and change someone's diaper. Sometimes the attachment within love is found in the decision to be patient and to help someone who is crying, even when you are very tired. Later in life, we trust that we are lovable because of these forgotten experiences. This certainty is what grounds us in relationships. Trust is built by love in our earliest years, and it is a subtle, invisible quality. But trust is as real as oxygen.

Attachment is an emotional tie grounded in trust.
Trust is what makes love stay.

I began to see how trust was difficult for me sometimes, through passages in my adult life. It has always been easy for me to host the notion that I was not really loved. Once, when I was working on my adoption issues, I actually asked Suzi if she thought my parents loved me.

She was incredulous, in a kind way. "Are you kidding, you silly man? Of course they love you! They are crazy about you!"

Her response led me to ask her another "adopted-kid question," because Suzi was the mother of two adopted children and had lived the experience of adoption as a parent.
I knew she understood what adoption was like for my parents in a personal way.

I asked her, "When did you first know that you loved Erika?"

She responded immediately, with words I had heard before. "I loved her from the first moment I got the phone call!"

My head started spinning. My own mother had said nearly the same words to me, many times, many years ago. My own mom had always told me, "We loved you from the first moment we saw you."

It began to dawn on me that my problem was not that I was unloved. I had been deeply loved as a child. My problem was that my ability to perceive love was a little impaired.

Sometimes, even when love is there, we can't feel it.

I had trouble with feeling, and love wasn't the only thing I couldn't feel. Sometimes when injury was present, I had trouble noticing that, too.

Being unconscious of our injuries from childhood is a little like Stockholm syndrome, where hostages eventually identify with and side with their own captors. This phenomenon was observed in the famous case of Patty Hearst, who was kidnapped and began to identify with her captors. She identified so strongly with them that she robbed banks with them. It is a strong part of our preservation instinct to identify with whoever we depend on. This is also why women in abusive relationships will defend the spouses who have hurt them. On some level, it feels like a betrayal for us to say how we have been wounded and by whom.

And yet, the only way to heal a wound is to acknowledge it. If we want to heal a wound, we have to enter it and understand it. Even if it feels like betrayal.

As I worked on all this in my attachment in therapy, I reported that I was never abused. But as I opened up, I found myself admitting there were wounds I had never noticed before.

For example, one key trigger came up repeatedly in my adult life. I always feel intense anger when I sense I am not being heard. I asked, "Could this be from being left in a crib in my preverbal years?"

Perhaps so. But I also began to see that some of my triggers could also stem from the culture of my parents' generation. Theirs was one that believed their prime directive was to instill moral values into their children. Just keeping us from going to hell was a touchdown. A parent was never meant to listen or discover who his or her children were or who he or she wanted to be. Such was the case in my home.

When I was an adult in my forties, after my third divorce, my dad certainly knew when to put on his preacher hat. My most recent crisis was a perfect opportunity to attempt another rescue of my soul. When I sat alone in another postdivorce empty house, he asked, "How could you be so selfish?"

Dad lived in a small town and was a leader in a conservative church. Everyone knew he had a son who was a little challenged in the morality department. My inability to stay married probably didn't reflect too well on our family in that world either.

As I worked in attachment therapy, I began to see that I longed for respect from my dad as a fellow adult. In this area of my life, I was still a kid to him, and I was probably an embarrassing little kid at that.

I knew he loved me, but I also knew I was living with something hurtful. I wrote and talked about this in therapy. I said hello to my feelings around not being seen and around not being heard. As I grew to accept and enter this part of my wound, I realized I needed to respond to him. I became ready to create a small boundary. I was ready to stand up for myself.

One day, I took a risk and shared what I had been struggling with.

> Dear Dad,
> Just like you, I have struggled with a few things in life. I am a human being who has been through some tough experiences, and I have tried to get better through treatment centers, therapist offices, AA meetings, and churches. I have stood up to face my issues and have taken responsibility for my decisions as an adult. I don't blame you for my illnesses, and

I don't expect you to fix anything for me either. How about
a little respect? Give me a break: I am your peer as an adult.
I love you,
Greg

My dad, who was in his late seventies at that time, heard me. He
saw the truth of what I was trying to get at, and he actually asked for
my forgiveness. Our exchange completely shifted our relationship
for the rest of the years together. I learned that I could be heard.
Unexpectedly, I felt empowered. A few weeks later, I went to my
boss and asked for (and received) an overdue raise.

When we heal and become whole, we are not brand-new. In our
wholeness, there remains a lattice of little cracks that are now
sealed, and they are where we have become stronger. When old
triggers heal, they remain for life, even though they dim in sensitivity. Jung once said, "I'd rather be whole than good."

The personal work I did during that dark passage was also like entering a cocoon. I felt like Stripe, in his dark, lonely, quiet place.
Inside the cocoon, the caterpillar's body dissolves so that it can
become something new. Liquefaction precedes metamorphosis. If
we want to become something new, then the old form has to go.

I became comfortable with other wounds from childhood. I could
now admit how I had been abandoned and my sense of trust had
once been broken. But I could also see how I was loved. I thought
about Suzi and her love for her adopted daughter and my own
mother's identical words about me. Even when I couldn't feel it as
a kid, I was still loved. As I worked, I allowed myself to feel the love
that was present in my childhood.

As I began to emerge from the cocoon of attachment therapy, I experimented with a new way of moving. I stepped into the air with my glistening wings and stood with a sense of responsibility. No one else could create my next reality. Loving attachment was my decision to make, even though this seemed unfamiliar. Love was really about deciding to trust.

Suzi and I have been together for over twelve years. We have partnered to help each other grow, and we have worked hard to help each other get to the next level. We both respect each other's work, even though our personal work differs in many ways. But one remarkable thing about our relationship is how the level of trust has grown between us. Through countless shared experiences and through every crisis, I have learned I can really count on her.

Once, on my birthday, we had an argument. I had stayed up late and failed to come to bed the night before, because I'd been drawn into a documentary I had found on cable TV. The next morning, Suzi expressed her discomfort about my delayed return to bed. She told me she had waited for me to come upstairs to bed. I tried to defend myself, explaining my actions.

She replied that I had not heard her. The tenor of our argument rose. I felt myself getting angry. I could feel her anger. I was triggered. She was not *hearing* me. She was triggered, too, and our argument became a crisis. I tried to apologize and explain. Nothing worked. The day dragged on, as we tried to decide what to do. Finally, we agreed to go forward with our plan for my birthday: we would drive in the car for two hours to a nearby mountain resort and spend the night in the hotel.

We spent a tense day at the resort, tried to hike, and tried to have dinner together, but nothing seemed to work. That night, I apologized again from the heart and admitted that I was triggered. I told her I felt like I wasn't being heard and that not being heard was an old trigger from my childhood. It was a trigger from my unexplored room.

When I was able to admit to why I felt so bad, Suzi connected with me. She replied, "I felt the same way when your parents lived with us. I can see why you would feel like that with me...I can see how no one heard you, when you were little."

I fractured with her affirmation of what was so painful inside me. When I was finally able to be vulnerable with Suzi, I experienced generosity. Suzi told me later that, in that moment, what mattered most to her was to relax into love. Love is our natural state, if only we can only relax into it.

My perspective about our argument that day has shifted over the years. I now can certainly see how our pattern of being in victimhood and then coming to the other's rescue played out on that day. We have worked extensively on learning about the drama triangle that develops between the victim, the rescuer, and the aggressor. We also now use a style of nonviolent communication, and we no longer blame the other for our emotions. We take responsibility for our own feelings and don't need to rescue each other. Everything has changed. But I would not have learned any of this if I had not stayed. Neither would Suzi.

Some people hold that we attract partners who have familiar energies and we are drawn to the familiar behaviors of our childhood families. For example, Harville Hendrix teaches that repair of our old injuries is the very heartbeat of long-term relationships. We attract partners with an unconscious hope that we can complete our unfinished business. If I have unfinished business with my mother, I will probably attract someone who reminds me of her. If my partner has unfinished work with her father, she will probably attract someone who reminds her of him.

My mentor has another way of expressing this. He says that we live in a classroom planet and that the universe often draws two people together in order for them to learn something important from each other. Sometimes this becomes a long-term relationship.

This chapter started with the question, "How do you make love stay?" But if we are honest, then we must admit there are times when love really should not stay. For example, in a scenario where one is endangered by an abusive partner, leaving the relationship can be the most courageous and spiritual thing anyone can do. If a spouse is in relationship with a partner in active addiction who is unwilling to recover, then ending the relationship may be the most positive thing that could happen. For either of them. Sometimes love should not stay.

It takes time and wisdom to discern what is trying to happen. The clarity about what is wrong with a relationship dawns slowly. Leaving in a good way can occur only when consciousness and clarity emerge from our personal work.

If life is really a classroom planet, then the classes in the "long-term relationship department" of this university are the most difficult ones offered. Sometimes we give up and drop them, because the work is so painful. Sometimes we go underground and live a detached, anesthetized existence with a partner we dislike. But the coursework in the LTR department tends to repeat itself, no matter who our partner is. The universe is patient. If we don't learn our lesson with this marriage, we will get another chance in the next marriage. And our next chance will be more costly.

But the flip side of the coin is that mastering even a little of this material can be the most exhilarating and profound experience we will ever have.

Aristotle taught about three kinds of friendship, which are really three phases seen in long-term relationships. He said friendships start as relationships based on casual, shared pleasure. They are an intersection between chemistry and fun but are no deeper than that.

Relationships may grow to a utilitarian friendship, where each person brings the skills and attributes the other needs. Opposites attract. This is the next inevitable phase of LTRs, when friendship deepens.

But there is a third, more profound phase of the LTR that Aristotle called the "completed friendship." This is what happens when one partner sees and appreciates the good in the other and only wants what is good for the other. They want the good, for the other's sake. Unconsciously, we have agreed to help each other heal. Healing is a fiber found in the tapestry of LTRs, if they mature.

Aristotle's completed friendship is the opposite of the question posed by Tom Robbins. If we ask how to make love stay, then we are really asking from a position of victimhood. Perhaps love will leave us. If love leaves us, then we are victims of love (even if we contributed to its demise). If love is gone, we prefer to think it is not our fault. We have been wronged.

In completed friendship, Aristotle asks instead, "What will happen to love, if we stay?"
What will happen if we stay because we want the good, for the other's sake?

It seems to me that if we are really crazy about someone and wonder if we could ever reach this level of connection with them, then it would be wise for us to allow a few questions of another kind to surface:

Are we with someone who also cares about personal growth?
Are we with someone who works on their own stuff, too?
Do we see the good in them?
Are we willing to help them find the good within themselves?
Are they willing to do this for us?

If we choose to stay, then we should be prepared. They will absolutely trigger us, and we will trigger them. We will each bring up the other's stuff from our respective unexplored rooms. There will be joy, and there will be pain.

But we can move through the pain, if we choose to stay present. This is what the practice of trust looks like.

If we stay, then love will stay.

Reflection

Create a quiet moment in a quiet place. Sit comfortably with your feet on the floor and your back straight, if you can. Breathe in deeply, and then exhale fully. Do this again, until you notice your body beginning to relax.

As you move into this relaxed space, allow your heart to settle.

Have you been able to make love stay?
Have you lived in a revolving door of one relationship after another?

Have your relationships ever felt stuck?
Has your current relationship become lifeless, but you stay anyway?

Have you repeatedly found yourself with someone who triggers you?
Have you found yourself attracting an abusive or controlling partner?

Do you feel weary of these patterns in your life?
Does a partnership to grow and heal sound like a breath of fresh air?
Does finding the good in someone call to you?

Does work on your side of the street seem worth it to you?
If this is so, then it is no coincidence that you sit with these words right now.

Take another deep breath and drop further into your heart.
Would you like to love deeper?
Do you have the willingness to stay?

Breathe in deeply, and then breathe out deeply.
Open your eyes when you are ready to come back to the room where you are sitting.

Chapter Eight

The Rewrite

I've been working on my rewrite, that's right
I'm gonna change the ending
Gonna throw away my title
And toss it in the trash

—PAUL SIMON

In Annie Proulx's brilliant novel *The Shipping News*, a man named Quoyle takes a job as a newspaper writer in a small town on the coast of Newfoundland. Quoyle's life is a mess. His wife, Petal, is dead, and he is raising their daughter, Bunny, as a single parent. Quoyle has not found his voice in life. He has not been able to tell Bunny that her mother has died. He does not have the voice to set boundaries for himself, either at work or in his relationships. Ironically, he takes a job as a newspaper reporter. His task seems to be to find his voice.

One of Quoyle's teachers is Billy, the seasoned reporter of the *Gammy Bird* newspaper. In an early scene, Billy tries to teach Quoyle about what a news headline is. He tells Quoyle that the headline is really the center of a story—the "beating heart of it." He believes that "what really makes a reporter" is the choice of a headline. He invites Quoyle to practice making up punchy, dramatic headlines. Billy then points to the dark clouds on the horizon and asks Quoyle to make up a headline.

Quoyle answers, "Horizon Fills with Dark Clouds?"

Billy shakes his head and corrects him: "Imminent Storm Threatens Village."

Quoyle responds, "But what if no storm comes?"

Billy shrugs and replies, "Village Spared from Deadly Storm."

As Quoyle begins to find his voice, he notices something in his un-explored room. It is the headlines of a story he has been repeating to himself. They are headlines to his own story. It starts to dawn on him that life follows the headlines we have created for ourselves.

Quoyle knows the Quoyle family originated in this remote part of Newfoundland. He moves his daughter and his aunt into the old Quoyle homestead on a rocky point overlooking the ocean, only to learn that the Quoyles of the nineteenth century were actually pi-rates, who lured ships onto the rocks in order to kill their crews and loot their supplies. He is living in a house built by pirates.

He also learns that his own father sexually molested his aunt when she was a child. In some ways, it seems that Quoyle has been un-knowingly carrying the shame of his family's heritage. In order to heal, Quoyle has to understand and transcend the dark roots of his past. His family's misdeeds also lay unexamined within his unexplored room. Quoyle's very name is a play on words, because his life is like a tangled coil of rope.

In the final chapter, a strong wind takes down the family house and leaves nothing but the stakes at the corners. But by this time, Quoyle has learned to speak for himself. He has told Bunny the truth about her mother. He has found his voice in the newspaper room. He has found his voice in a new relationship.

As he looks at the wreckage of his house, he creates a new headline: "Deadly Storm Takes House. Leaves Excellent View." Quoyle has begun to rewrite his life.

When I was early in my journey, my mentor asked me to do a rewrite of my own headlines. He called his exercise the "soul covenant." He gave me a list of questions to consider, and they turned my life upside down as I sat with the answers that surfaced: Why did you choose your parents? What did your soul come here to learn?

There is a Jungian tradition that we choose our parents before birth. This is an antidote to victimhood. If we have chosen our own difficult life circumstances and suffering, then they become our responsibility. They are what we needed in order to fulfill our purpose. In this lens, our purpose might be thought of as a "soul covenant," a promise we have made to ourselves.

In a men's retreat, James Hillman once recounted the story of Manolete, a legendary Spanish bullfighter who seemed timid as a boy. He hid behind his mother's apron. Hillman commented that perhaps Manolete knew it was his destiny to face a thousand-pound black bull and become a renowned bullfighter. Perhaps this was the reason Manolete chose a mother with a great apron to hide behind—he was preparing for his life-and-death battle behind a cape.

Of course, his soul covenant questions were based on the premise that our lives have meaning, in a mystical sense. They assume we are here for a purpose and can discover it, if we are quiet enough. Is it possible this is true? Have we all come into existence to learn something?

My mentor's questions stimulated me to look at my own story. As I entered my own unexplored room back then, I found some news-paper clippings with headlines about me. My first headline read, "Boy Abandoned by Mother, Adopted by Religious Couple." Scratch the surface of these headlines, and you will find a victim. Underneath these words are misalignment, abandonment, and loss.

But there is another way of looking at our seminal events. Jean Shinoda Bolen points out that "not everyone who has been a victim has been victimized." Sometimes inside our trauma, we may find our strength. We can refuse to be dominated by our trauma.

I started my mentor's exercise and imagined that before I was born, I chose my biological mother (and father) because I needed their genetic strengths. I imagined that I chose to be an adopted kid, because I needed to experience being abandoned. I needed to become more sensitive to heart connection. My sensitivity to heart connection would become my core strength in life. My wound be-came my strength.

As I looked at my life in this new way, I imagined that I chose this particular adopted family for a reason. Perhaps I would experience love and connection, along with some cultural shame and dysfunction that I needed to transcend and heal. Other wounds became my other strengths.

As I sat with my exercise, my old story no longer fit. I was going to have to create a new headline for my journey. The next version read, "Wounded Healer Explores His Roots."
The subtext of this headline was responsibility and choice. There was no victim any longer. Instead, there was a hint of purpose and meaning.

Purpose and meaning were something I grew up with a sense of. My adoptive parents belonged to a conservative, fundamentalist protestant church, where purpose and meaning were central. There was no higher calling than to be a missionary for the church. When I was little, I learned that everyone had a mission, which was to bring our religious teachings to the whole world. Growing up, I was pretty proud of my religious understanding. It set me apart. I was a proud fundamentalist.

When I was young, I even imagined that perhaps I should become a minister. In my first year of college, I was a theology major. I studied biblical Greek and was a church leader. As college progressed, I was torn between theology and my first love: medicine. I eventually talked to my adviser, an elderly, southern chemistry professor, about it. I explained to him that I was torn between being a pastor and going to medical school. I asked him what I should do.

He looked at me kindly, and after a long pause, he smiled and replied, "Just do something useful."

I switched to premed.

I had a lot to learn about what was really useful. And his simple advice was deeper than I could imagine at that moment. Usefulness isn't about ego or recognition. Usefulness is about being ordinary. A useful simple tool at the right moment can save the day. For me these days, my own sense of usefulness is about how I connect with other human beings, one at a time.

A few years later in medical school, I was still a fervent believer. I studied the Bible and wrote religious songs for church. I looked for openings to talk to people about my faith. There can be a darker side to religiosity, of course.

For me, the darker side was how I took a harsh view of anyone who deviated from my standard of moral behavior. A moral perch like this can be a real power trip. For example, one of my med-school teachers was a former church member. It was rumored that he had divorced his wife, married a nonbeliever, and left our church. When I heard this story, I was certain my professor needed to be rescued.

It wasn't long before my own life unfolded in an ironic (and predictable) way. When I was an intern on my surgery rotation, I had a surprising interruption. One afternoon, I was called out of surgery in my scrubs to find the deputy sheriff waiting to serve me with divorce papers. A few weeks later, I came out of surgery again to meet a couple of elders from my church. They had decided my activities were not acceptable, and they asked if they could remove my name from the list of church members. I said yes.

My moral perch was gone. I wasn't going to be the one to rescue my professor or anyone else. I was divorced, remarried with a non-believer, and out of the church.
By then, a fracture between me and the religion of my childhood seemed complete. I had felt like a phony and only wanted to find some way to become authentic. I blamed the religion of my parents for what was wrong with me.

I could no longer believe my church was the only group which understood the world correctly. I went to cultural war and made a conscious decision to bury my religious traditions in my unexplored room. They were forgotten and denied.

In our religious subculture, shellfish and pork were not allowed. Alcohol and smoking were not permitted. Extramarital, premarital, and gay sex were unthinkable. I grew up with religious teachers who discouraged theater attendance, card playing, dancing, and rock and roll. When I was finally dismissed from church membership, I resolved to do my best to smoke, drink, dance, eat shrimp, attend movies, have sex, and play rock and roll. My rebound didn't work so well for me.

About one year after my departure from my church, I drank so much that I found myself in treatment for alcoholism and chemical dependency. But I was undeterred. Religion was still evil and remained buried downstairs. For decades, I opposed all church-related things. I disliked all religions. Comedian Rowen Atkinson has proposed that there is a special circle in hell for those who have watched Monty Python's lampoon of the Christian advent, called *The Life of Brian*. I went further than this. As a young father, I used to screen the *Life of Brian* video on Easter for my kids. No doubt there is a special circle within Atkinson's circle for someone like me.

In the world of personal work, if we look at what we hate, we can learn much about what lies unseen in our own interior. When we talk about how evil a liberal or a conservative is, we are really projecting a part of ourselves on to someone else. When I imagined being judged and rejected by the conservative members of my church, I failed to see something important. I had also been judging myself. There was a part of *me* that had been intolerant. There was a big part of *me* that was afraid of "the other." There was an intolerant fundamentalist living in my basement.

In my late forties, I sat beneath the Colorado Rockies in a restaurant with my former high-school girlfriend, and I made disparaging remarks about my religious upbringing. I shared my projections about where I had come from. I hated the imagined religious hypocrisy I'd been a part of when I was young. Her reply shocked me to my core.

Suzi looked into my eyes and softly said, "I remember the goodness and kindness that were inside you. I remember your big heart for people. I think that you are trying to find that person again."

It seemed like the earth stopped at that moment. I looked up at the mountains above Breckinridge and felt the tears come up. I could see she was right. On some level, I had been estranged from my own core. There was a vital part of me that I had discarded.

As I did the work of rewriting my headlines, I found something surprising. Here was a fundamentalist, sitting on the front pew of the church of my childhood. He was in my unexplored room, right where I'd left religion.

From an early age, I had always sensed that the world was a kind and loving place and that we were cared for by a supreme being. Without a supreme being, my current worldview had become a little more hostile and chaotic. I was beginning to comprehend that I was missing something I wanted to recover.

On the other hand, the religious worldview of my childhood no longer fit very well. I had imagined that people who didn't share my beliefs were untrustworthy and perhaps evil. This was the opposite of my heart's experience as an adult. Some of the most loving and trustworthy people I had ever known were completely nonreligious or had belief systems that were completely different than what I had grown up with.

When I was young, I pictured the religious practices of my church as the only way of finding spirituality. I had believed it was spiritual to ignore my feelings. But as my life unfolded, I had learned that this was an unhealthy and impossible practice. I had learned that to follow my heart was the most spiritual thing I could ever do. So much of what I had believed as a child was untrue.

This is a dilemma all of us face when we become adults, no matter what we have been taught growing up. In one way, childhood can be thought of as a pure way of looking at the world. Everyone is a fundamentalist at age eight. We hold on to concrete explanations for everything. There is no room for mystery or paradox. When we are children, we have no way of holding mystery and paradox. As we mature, we usually outgrow simple, pure ways of looking at things. Our childhood maps of life no longer fit so well. This is because life is actually more complicated than what we could have imagined. Experience trumps ideas, just as a landscape trumps a map. Life always wins. It seems as if life invites us to be messy, and then to find our center.

I think this might be a reason we fundamentalists feel anger welling up when we first interact with the secular world. If our childhood premises no longer function so well, the world is scary.

"Why did you choose your parents? What did your soul come here to learn?" As I sat with my mentor's questions, I found myself looking at the abandoned church in my basement. I felt a desire to rewrite this part of my life and faced a dilemma. I could not regress to the simple worldview of my childhood. But how could I reclaim the good I had left behind?

I decided to experiment by physically reentering the doors of my old church. I was drawn to participate in a physical ceremony, to see if I could regain what I had lost. Baptism is a Christian tradition that uses water to symbolize letting go of an old life, and embracing a new one. I decided to be rebaptized, to the delight of my elderly parents. To them, I was returning to "The Truth." To me, it was a little more complicated than that.

For me, my rebaptism at age forty-eight offered me a ritual way to forgive myself. It was a way of acknowledging and loving the fundamentalist part of myself, sitting in my unexplored room. It was about viewing my own tribe (and their intolerance toward me) with some compassion too. I began to remember a few reasons I had loved my path so much in the first place. My ceremony of reentry allowed for me to reclaim parts of myself that I had buried.

Through the lens of the soul covenant exercise, I began to see that I had chosen to land in this conservative church for some specific reasons. There were many wonderful things here that I needed for my journey. I inherited the genetics of alcoholism from both biological parents. In order to survive, I needed to grow up in an alcohol- and drug-free home, for as long as possible. I also needed some kind of moral structure as I grew up. But most importantly, I think I needed to learn that the universe has meaning and is kind. This sense is a heart-level knowledge that propels me to do my work in the world. This gift of orientation came from my religious subculture. This is one reason why I chose my parents.

Someone recently asked me what my religion was, and I found myself replying that I am a nonobservant fundamentalist. I imagine this is much like being a nonobservant Jew. I no longer practice the cultural rules of my religion, in a strict sense. But I have love for where I have come from. I attend church from time to time and feel genuine connection with the people I grew up with.

One teaching I grew up with was the concept of a Sabbath observance, which is not unlike the Jewish notion of refraining from secular activities, from sundown on Friday night until sundown on Saturday. I don't keep Sabbath as a religious day, but I still try to give myself protected "downtime" to regenerate, enjoy walks in nature, and write.

As we grow as human beings, we become more complex. Ken Wilber points out that particles incorporate to become atoms, which join together to become molecules, and molecules then become cells. Cells join to become organs, and organs work together. We transcend all our small parts as we grow.

And inside our core, there is always something that defines function.

The molecule of hemoglobin is a long, folded protein that looks a little like a giant tangle of spaghetti, and it is a central component of our blood. It is what gives blood its red color and carries oxygen from our lungs to our tissues. Without hemoglobin, we die. At the center of this complex protein is one tiny atom: iron. Without iron, hemoglobin does not function and will not carry oxygen.

My religious training is like the iron atom inside hemoglobin. My sense of meaning and purpose came from this part of my past. This colors my function in the world.

By reentering this part of my past, I have reclaimed something that was always mine. When I recovered treasure from this corner of my unexplored room, I became richer and more complicated. In order for me to own my treasure, I had to be willing to rewrite the thing I had rejected. For me to incorporate my own shadow material back into my life, I needed a willingness to rethink my story.

Virginia Satir said, "I think if I have one message, one thing before I die that most of the world would know, it would be that the event does not determine how to respond to the event. That is a purely personal matter. The way in which we respond will direct and influence the event more than the event itself."

That day I was rebaptized, I wrote a new headline: "Fundamentalist Becomes Spiritual."

If you look at my rewrite from the outside, you might say it almost looks like the religious idea of forgiveness. Forgiveness is often symbolized by a physical action, like the baptism ceremony I am so grateful for. In the acclaimed 1983 film *The Mission*, Robert DeNiro plays a mercenary soldier named Rodrigo Mendoza, who experiences this.

Mendoza has made a brutal living by kidnapping and selling South American Guaraní natives into slavery. Mendoza reaches a crisis in his life when he is betrayed by his fiancée and then commits a murder. He sinks into depression. In his despair, he is visited by Jesuit Father Gabriel, who challenges Mendoza to undertake a suitable penance for his violent, unconscious life.

Mendoza accompanies the Jesuits on their journey to the Jesuit Guaraní mission, up into the mountains. His penance is to drag a heavy bundle behind him, containing his armor, his sword, and remnants of his old life. He climbs the final rocky cliff with painful exhaustion and finally kneels at the top, exhausted. He is pressed to the ground by the heavy weight on his back. He looks up. A young native man, perhaps one whose father Mendoza killed in the past, approaches, and they look at each other. The native bends down toward Mendoza with his sword in hand. Instead of striking Mendoza, he swings his sword to cut loose the heavy sack that weighs Mendoza to the earth. Their eyes connect. The native man has become part of the Jesuit community. He has committed an act of generosity. He has rewritten his past.

For Mendoza, his own weight has been released. He weeps and is embraced with silent forgiveness. A powerful rewrite has been passed forward to him.
And I know how he feels.

When my first wife and I divorced, my son was nine months old. She moved across the United States with him, over two thousand miles away, so she could be near her family. My son grew up with my parents nearby, but he only saw me once a year. It was a difficult way for him to grow up, even though I tried to be in his life.

Twenty-four years later, he asked me to attend his wedding. I arrived to support the ceremony, but at the rehearsal dinner, he announced to the group that his grandfather was like the father he'd never had. I was crushed, but I knew it was true. After the wedding was over, I went back my motel room, alone. I wept. And then the phone rang. My son had called me from his honeymoon.

I told him I knew he'd had a difficult life growing up without me and that I could hear his truth at the rehearsal dinner. We had indeed been unconnected, as father and son. I told him I was sorry.
He asked me a question that made my heart leap: "Would you like to start over?"

"Yes!" I replied, through the tears.

And today, my son and I have grown close. We talk every week, and our lives are deeply connected as men. My past has been rewritten through his powerful act of generosity. Like Mendoza, I have experienced the power of rewrite.

In Aristotle's writings on friendship, he refers to a virtuous quality of being magnanimous. Being magnanimous means being "intelligently generous" with an adversary or someone of weaker standing. Even though being magnanimous traditionally involves how we treat someone else, I think it is also possible for us to be magnanimous with ourselves.

Such generosity poured upon ourselves has the power to release negative emotions that are tightly bound to us. It is ironic that mere generosity transforms the most rejected objects in our unexplored room.

In my experience, generosity depends on how we relanguage our past. This is what leads us to take actions that contain forgiveness.

Suppose I have caused an injury or made a foolish decision that turned into a hurtful action that I now regret. If I look into my past and say, "This was the best I could have done with my abilities, my knowledge, and my beliefs at that time," then I have been magnanimous with myself.

Generosity has arrived. From our standpoint in the present moment, we know much more now than we did in the past. Our previous self is a weaker self, in this sense. Our past self is a person to whom generosity can be offered.

One result of such generosity is release. This is what can be so powerful behind creating some kind of ritual for ourselves. The action of ritual engages all of our five senses, and we experience it from the heart. For example, in my own rewrite work, I have written down old resentments on a scrap of paper to burn on the shore of the Oregon coast. With a little homemade ceremony, my old sadness dissipated and regret evaporated. Release happens naturally, with dramatization.

Generosity alters the way we see others. If we ever start to recognize ourselves in others, we will notice that their humanity matches our own humanity in surprising ways—especially anyone who has done us harm. If we have done the best *we* could do, at the moment, *then perhaps so did they.* If we can say they also did the best they could do, then the negative emotions of our own judgment about them will evaporate.

We all have a capacity to see others with gentleness. This is not easy work. But it is a work that is possible in our unexplored room, because this is the space where our fondest projections of others are held. Our old judgments from the past actually hold on to us tightly, unless we look at them with neutrality. These judgments often contain the very flaws found concealed in our own identity.

Once, I found myself saying farewell to a city that had been my home for twenty years. This was a place of great joy, where my daughters had been born. It was also a place of pain and drama, where among other things, my divorces had occurred. As with most divorces, there was mutually assured injury. Hurtful things had been said and done to me, and I had said and done hurtful things as well.

Over the years that had passed, I had explored my own motives. As I worked with the material in my unexplored room, I had to own my own anger, betrayal, and fear. We are all just human beings, after all. At times, we all have to see the real imperfections in ourselves and our partners. We have to compare how we imagined ourselves to be in a relationship with how we really showed up in the relationship. Over the years, I had tried to make restitution for my own unwellness. But as I prepared to leave the city, I realized I still carried traces of sadness, resentment, and regret from those years. I wanted to rewrite this part of my story.

One evening, I decided to make another ritual for myself. I drove to former residences where I had lived or stayed and stopped my car in the darkness at each place for a few minutes. I blessed each house as I sat at the curb. I found myself silently thanking those people who had been a part of my past life. I wanted to be generous with myself and with them.

I could now see that I did the best I could have done at that time. So did they.
I made peace with the good and bad of the past. I allowed the release of negative emotions from my old memories. I allowed the anger to release, if it surfaced. I released the sadness and regret when it said hello. With my little ritual in the car, I was rewriting my own past. This rewrite also changed my unexplored room and how I felt about what was there.

David Whyte observes that "To regret fully is to appreciate how high the stakes are in even the average human life. Fully experienced, regret turns our eyes attentive and alert to a future possibly lived better than our past."

Regret directs us to repair our mistakes, and it schools us.

I have found that an honest rewrite does not take away my errors or the wisdom that came from my mistakes. Rewriting, however, does create gratitude where it is least expected. Rewriting has made me grateful for who I am so far and for everyone who has walked with me.

My latest headline is this: "Thanks."

Reflection

Make yourself comfortable in a quiet place. Listen to the quiet.
If there is sound, take it in, and then release it.
If thoughts come to you, breathe them in. Release them as you breathe out.
Breathe in slowly at your own pace, and then breathe out.

Allow your body to relax.
Feel the quiet, open space. You are in a safe place.
Allow yourself to drift in time.

Allow yourself to drift backward, before the moment of your birth.
Drift backward before the moment of your conception.

Imagine all the places and times you could choose from.
Imagine you could have been born anywhere, to any family, in any culture…
Can you imagine why you might have chosen this one?

Can you imagine how your work might have been served by your beginning?
Could there be a reason you have chosen this path?

Are there childhood beliefs or teachings to be found in your unexplored room?
Is this a chapter that can be rewritten?
Could there be treasure within your discarded material?

Is there regret that comes up for things you wish you could have changed?

Greg Loewen

Did any old injuries surface for you, where someone has hurt you?
Are there feelings of sadness or resentment that say hello to you?

It is possible for you to relanguage our past.
        It is possible to rewrite your life.

Are there old wounds that are ready for release?

Breathe in slowly, and then breathe out.
Open your eyes and return to the room.

Chapter Nine
Taboo Tattoo

*I don't trust my inner feelings
'cause my inner feelings come and go*

—LEONARD COHEN

Somewhere in the darkest portion of our unexplored room, we are vaguely conscious of an embarrassing object. It is something we would never bring up in conversation. We instinctively sense that other people would find our object unacceptable too. Perhaps they would say something judgmental about us. They probably would look away and change the subject to something nice.

There is some shame around this object, and it isn't only our shame. It is everyone else's shame too. If we had the capacity to look inside their unexplored rooms, I guarantee we would find the very same object hiding there too. In fact, this objectionable item would probably show up in the unexplored room of virtually everyone we know in our society. This object is taboo.

Taboo refers to what is forbidden or unacceptable in the view of the group. Often, it was a behavior that was forbidden in order to promote survival of the group. The definition of *taboo* changes between cultures and societies. In 1934, Cole Porter wrote this:

In olden days, a glimpse of stocking
was looked on as something shocking.
Now heaven knows!
Anything goes!

In some religious groups, divorce and remarriage are considered taboo. In our society at large, many sexual behaviors are proscribed. Criminal sex offenses are an example of taboo in our culture. In the United States, convicted sex offenders are sentenced to a life of being ostracized. Once they are released from prison, they are compelled to register with authorities wherever they live. But there is another common taboo that ostracizes and segregates members of our society in a completely different way.

Mental illness remains a taboo throughout most of our culture.

When I was a boy, a Missouri senator named Thomas Eagleton became the vice-presidential running mate for George McGovern. When it became nationally known that he had been treated for depression, his candidacy was completely derailed, and he was dropped from the electoral ticket. Mental illness was a taboo back in 1972, and in many ways, it still is.

In casual conversation, if we ever disclose that we have struggled with mental illness or have ever attempted suicide, the conversation will take a sharp left turn. Disclosure can be dangerous for our future, and the conversation is no longer casual. It has become intimate. This is because we hold issues like mental illness, despair, and suicide as deeply personal. These issues still hold a quality of taboo for most of us. In the subculture I grew up in, it was widely held that depression (and other mental illnesses) was really a sign of spiritual failure. There was judgment around mental illness: "If you are depressed, then you aren't very spiritual, are you?"

The term *illness* can have different implications. Sometimes, it implies impairment. The psychological symptoms of anxiety, for example, might be universal. But if your anxiety prevents you from doing what you really want to do, then it is an impairment and an illness.

If we look at mental illness from this perspective, we might have to agree with Stephen King, who said, "I think that we're all mentally ill. Those of us outside the asylums only hide it a little better—and maybe not all that much better after all."

When we say someone is "ill," another implication is that it is not his or her fault. Being sick is usually a kind of thing that happens *to* us. When illness happens, science studies the illness. It invites us to suspend any judgment about the person and look at what makes him or her sick, in an objective way. It has been historic for us to blame illness on lifestyle, if it is at all possible to do so. Blame and shame can be a part of what maintains the taboo status of (at least some) illnesses.

Consider the idea of morbid obesity. It is an illness, but it is also another common taboo. We hesitate to speak about someone's obesity because of taboo. We say their obesity is impolite to talk about.

Taboos are always about shame. But morbid obesity is a disease that affects over six million people in the United States and contributes to secondary illnesses such as heart disease, diabetes, and cancer. It is a disease where medical and surgical intervention can be lifesaving.

This particular taboo comes with a shaming message that obesity equals a lack of self-control. We hear, "How could they do that to themselves? If only they would eat healthfully, then they would lose weight..."

These remarks imply there is no illness; there is only a lack of self-control. But science clearly shows that the issues around obesity are much more complex than commonly imagined. While diet and sedentary lifestyle are important, genetic, metabolic, and medical factors (such as medications and hormonal status) also play key roles in the development of morbid obesity.

If we choose instead to think of our obesity as an illness, then our condescending judgment can be suspended. It is no longer a personal failure. It is not a moral failure. It is only a disease that requires treatment.

In order for those of us with morbid obesity to seek treatment, we have to view ourselves with a little compassion. Treatment is a form of self-care, requiring compassion for the self. Changing behavior is a form of self-care. Our own self-care requires that we erase negative judgments we have made about ourselves. We have to erase the judgments others have made about us too.

If we have morbid obesity and begin to view our condition as an illness, it is easier for us to ask for help. *Webster* defines *illness* as a specific condition that prevents the body or mind from working. When we internalize the understanding that we are not bad and that we only have a *condition*, we discover that there is a profound knowledge base, expertise, and treatment available for our condition. Treatment for the illness of obesity includes recovery groups and the medical specialty of bariatrics. With the observation that we are ill, we neutralize stigma and taboo to open a door of action for ourselves.

When I was a young psychiatry resident, I was taught that mental illness was just another illness, like heart disease or diabetes. This was the area of medicine I hoped to specialize in. I was also taught about suicide. We learned that it was normal for many human beings to have thoughts of suicide. It is estimated that as many as eight million have thoughts of suicide each year.

We also learned that suicide itself was taboo and that thoughts of suicide were something most people are reluctant to voluntarily admit to. We learned that if you ask certain patients if they have had suicidal thoughts, sometimes the dam would burst. The person who is hiding his or her private struggle with suicide may find great relief when it's finally possible to talk about it without being judged. He or she can finally share his or her inner battle. This can happen when someone is able to listen in a kind and nonjudgmental way. It is our job to break taboo and to enter the zone of the forbidden. Our task is to ask the question.

We were also taught that suicidal thoughts were a function of how badly someone feels about his or her life. The more psychic pain we experience, the more we want it to end. Our pain, if it is in the form of despair, may seem unresolvable. In the face of this kind of pain, it is normal for us to think about how we might end it. Sometimes, our only option seems like it might be self-destruction. We learned that when we are in a severe personal crisis, fleeting thoughts of suicide are normal for anyone.

Suicidal risk is a vital sign mental-health caregivers take, just like temperature and blood pressure. We are taught to ask questions like these:

- Have you had thoughts of suicide?
- Have you made a plan to harm yourself?
- Have you thought about how you might do this?
- Have you taken any steps to carry out your plan?
- Have you ever tried to harm yourself in the past?

What happened to you that has made you want to end your life?

For someone who is actively contemplating suicide, answering questions like these may be lifesaving. Talking about it may come as a relief. Most people who are thinking about suicide want to find a way to live. It can be a release to finally tell someone how intolerable their life has become. The answers to these questions can also help to identify who is at the highest risk of harming themselves. This is what opens the door for lifesaving intervention.

Experiencing the suicide of a patient is a wound many psychiatrists and physicians share. I remember sitting in my psychiatry-division chair's office one day. The family arrived. With my boss, we all went up to the roof of the psychiatry building together. This was an exercise in grief for all of us. We went over to the edge to see where my patient had jumped off the roof.

One of my friends in the emergency department had been on duty for the attempted resuscitation, and he was with my patient at the final moments. When he described the scene of my patient's death, I was broken with grief. For years, I asked myself if I could have done or said anything differently that might have prevented his death. Mine was only a small fraction of the family's pain. But this is pain we all share when someone chooses to leave the planet through suicide. It might seem that my experience in psychiatry would have been enough to prevent me from ever considering suicide myself. Well, not completely.

Perhaps some of my lowest moments in life came when I was in early recovery from alcoholism and addiction. During my first year of recovery, my marriage ended. I lived alone in a small apartment in a poor neighborhood. I was going to AA meetings every day.

One day, I went to a speaker meeting. The speaker, as she talked about her recovery, also talked about her struggle with depression. In front of the entire group of a hundred or so alcoholics, she admitted that she had recurrent suicidal thoughts. Every day, she had thought about killing herself. She was even imagining how she might do it. She went to her psychiatrist and told on herself. She blew herself in.

Her psychiatrist gently replied, "This is not normal. It is not normal to imagine how you might end your life, every day. This is your depression speaking to you."

She made the decision to accept his help for her depression.

At that moment, the lights went on inside my head. Suicidal thoughts had been dominating my daily life too. But suicide was a taboo concealed within my unexplored room. I had been taught by society, "Don't talk about that!" For example, it is commonly held that talking about suicide makes it more likely to happen. I couldn't even admit that my own suicidal thoughts existed.

When I heard this courageous woman tell her story, I was shocked, because I recognized my own story in hers. I too had been living with the same sense of despair, as I drove back and forth to work on the highway. I had been in denial about my own suicidal ideas. I had been in denial about my own depression.

Mental illness is unique from other illnesses in some ways. One of the potential ways that it differs from other health conditions is that when we are mentally ill, our very perception of reality may change. When I was in active addiction, I had no idea that I had a problem with alcohol. Or drugs. I was in complete denial. It was impossible for me to sense what alcohol and drugs were doing to me.

Depression carried a similar impairment of my perceived reality. I could not imagine how I could ever be happy again. I struggled with feeling hopeless, even though I was young with a wonderful life ahead. I struggled with not feeling useful, even though I helped people every day at work and elsewhere. I loved my patients, but at times, I felt worthless as a doctor. I struggled to feel joy or rewards from my own work. I loved my kids, but I had been told I was worthless as a father. And I felt worthless in relationships, and I couldn't see what was happening to me.

Sometimes, our inner feelings don't correctly inform us about reality. Our inner feelings are transient. As Leonard Cohen put it, "inner feelings come, and inner feelings go." Zen Master Thich Nhat Hanh tells it another way in one of his most powerful teachings about our identity. He calls it "the mountain meditation." Hanh points out that most suicides, and especially the suicide of adolescents, could be prevented with this teaching.

In the mountain meditation, Hanh asks us to imagine ourselves as a great mountain that reaches above the clouds. Storm clouds come. There is rain. It passes. The mountain is still here. A blizzard comes, and there is tremendous wind, snow, and cold. It passes. The mountain is still here. The sun comes out, and the clouds separate. The mountain is still here. In this meditation, we learn that our emotions are like the weather. They come, and they go.

Our identity is the mountain. We are not the storm.
Hanh teaches that it is a mistake for us to identify with our storms.

How often have you caught yourself saying, "I am angry," instead of saying, "I feel anger?"

And what would it be like, if we were to ask, "Who is feeling the anger?" or "Who is feeling the sadness?"

We might say, "I am feeling sadness," or "I am feeling despair," instead of "I am depressed."

I sat with the realization that I was experiencing depression and became ready to ask for help. I saw a psychiatrist and started on an antidepressant. Night gradually turned into day. My perception changed. Over the months and years that followed, with medication and therapy, my life shifted. I started to feel a sense of hope. The depression I had experienced lifted.

What I began to realize, as my feelings of depression lifted, was that my perception had been impaired, because I had been identifying with my own emotions. I was not hearing my own voice; I was really hearing the voice of my illness. Depression had begun to interpret my life for me. It spoke to me, and I was listening.

When I think about how that AA speaker stood in front of all of us and admitted that she suffered from depression, it makes me want to cheer. What courage. What heart. She saved my life. When I think of how Betty Ford and others have gone public with their treatment for addiction, I am also grateful. When I first heard Brené Brown talk about her own vulnerability on TED Talks, I cried and cheered. As did everyone else. Millions of us. The taboo around being vulnerable is waning. And the taboo around mental illness is waning. The taboo around suicide is waning. The taboo around depression is waning.

In a study of more than eighty-seven thousand people in seventeen countries, Dr. Matthew Nock and his colleagues at Harvard estimated that almost 3 percent of humanity has, at one time or another, attempted suicide. In the United States, with a population of 310 million, 3 percent of the population means almost one million people. In 2016, the Centers for Disease Control reported that the American suicide rate has risen by 24 percent in the past fifteen years, which is the highest level in three decades. This brings the suicide fatality rate to over forty-two thousand people per year. Even though it has been kept secret, the despair that drives suicide has touched all of us.

But there is a new movement in society responding to this health crisis. In Seattle, one in four citizens knows CPR. If you fall to the ground with a cardiac arrest in Seattle, your odds of surviving are much higher there than anywhere else, because you are surrounded by ordinary citizens who have been trained to save your life. It turns out there is also a CPR for suicide. It is called QPR.

QPR is a kind of emergency mental-health intervention training designed for anyone who might be around someone who shows the warning signs of thinking about suicide. This could be a doctor, nurse, counselor, or health-care provider. But it could also easily be a family member, a friend, or an ordinary citizen who hears a warning sign. Anytime someone says things like "I just can't go on like this," or "My family would be better off without me," it is time for action. It is time for curiosity and sensitivity.

Over a million have been trained in QPR, which stands for "question, persuade, and refer." This technique teaches us to ask the right questions when someone expresses suicidal thoughts. It teaches that someone who is considering suicide is probably on the fence about going through with it. They want to find a way to live, and this is how the intervention of QPR saves lives. QPR is what happens when taboo goes away.

Taboo is something we hide from others and from ourselves. The opposite of a taboo is a tattoo, something we say about ourselves with ink and a story we tell about ourselves.

When my kids were teenagers, they wanted tattoos. I told them this was fine. I told them they had to tell the tattoo artist they did not have their father's permission to get a tattoo. And that I was a doctor. This worked for a while.

Greg Loewen

Like some people of my age, I have never been a tattoo fan, particularly. I have long associated tattoos with drunkenness, like the Jimmy Buffett song about margaritas, where he awakens to find he has "nothing to show but this brand-new tattoo / But it's a real beauty, / A Mexican cutie, how it got here / I haven't a clue."

In the era I grew up in, tattoos themselves were a mild taboo. Those with obvious tattoos might even find professional employment difficult to capture.

But like so many taboos of the past, this is another that seems to be no longer shocking. I have been learning this from my kids. Tattoo is now being reaffirmed in parts of our culture as a way to publicly display something true about what is inside of us. Instead of merely seeing someone's arm, we also might see a baby elephant. Instead of seeing someone's foot, we might see the word *imagine*. And we might learn something profound about who we are with.

Tattoo is also personal. It is something that (unless it is on our forehead) we may choose to reveal or not. And we may also choose to place the tattoo in a private place on our body, where revealing it is a kind of an act of intimacy.

Tattoo is permanent. Perhaps this is a reason why old people like me should be the only ones to get tattooed. By the time someone reaches my age, we have a much better idea of what image we are willing to be comfortable with for the rest of our lives—which is a much shorter period of time to worry about.

If it is done right, then the image might really say something true about who we are. It might be something we want to declare to the world. On the other hand, the tattoo might not really be about saying anything to anybody except ourselves. Tattoo might also only be a note to self, like a string on our finger. It is a way to remember something about our interior.

Years ago, my wife started her business for counseling and meditation, named "Northern Light," and her symbol was a beautiful eight-pointed star within a square, which was within a circle. Suzi recently attended a women's spiritual retreat in Glastonbury, United Kingdom, where a great crop circle had formed. The crop circle turned out to be beautiful; it consisted of an eight-pointed star within a square, within a circle. Suzi was moved and placed her little business card in the middle of the crop circle. Her retreat leader told her the crop circle had formed on the day Suzi had landed in the United Kingdom. Here was an image that meant something special to her.

When we were in Hawaii a few months later, Suzi confided to me that she had been considering her first tattoo. I was excited for her and replied that I had made a similar decision for myself. We found an amazing tattoo artist in Pahoa and gave her photos of the crop circle with a copy of Suzi's card. We came back the next week to see her and found that she had created an amazing likeness of the eight-pointed star. Suzi's body art found its place on her left lower leg, above her ankle. It was beautiful.

What was more beautiful, however, was how the tattoo changed Suzi. Her new tattoo inspired her to step into her own power in a different way. I noticed a subtle change in how she talked with strangers and in how she wrote about her work. Her body art was a beautiful symbol of her interior. She was proud for anyone to see it. Her body art said, "This is who I am." It was her new identity.

I also reached a decision to have my first tattoo while in Pahoa. But when you see my tattoo, you will see something completely different. It is a small semicolon on my left wrist.

I was once talking with a colleague at a national meeting when we noticed each other's tattoos. She also has a tiny semicolon tattooed on her wrist. We immediately laughed, hugged, and felt connected, because we both knew the meaning of the semicolon. Both my colleague and I were a part of the Project Semicolon movement. Project Semicolon proposes that if your life is a sentence, and your sentence concludes (because of mental illness, suicide, or addiction), then the end of your life could be grammatically represented by a period. But you can do something else with your sentence. You can get help. You can start your life over.

Amy Bleuel, a graphic artist who lost her father to suicide, started the courageous Project Semicolon in 2013. Project Semicolon explains, "A semicolon is used when an author could've chosen to end his or her sentence, but chose not to. The author is you, and the sentence is your life." Amy eventually lost her life to the disease of suicide that she battled for years. But her work lives on through ink-tinted skin, everywhere.

Project Semicolon symbolizes recovery, and when we meet our semicolon siblings, we feel like reunited survivors from an old plane crash. We instantly know one another like family, even if we have never met. We have all started a new sentence that says, "I want to work on my stuff."

My daughter was a psychiatric nurse at a university psychiatric-emergency department, where many of the caregivers had little semicolon tattoos. Imagine feeling desperate and afraid as you sit in a psychiatric ER, waiting to be seen. You are almost ready to bolt, but then the person who is caring for you reveals his or her semicolon tattoo to you. Suddenly, you realize the person who has been caring for you once sat where you now sit. You are being treated with unusual empathy and understanding because you are with someone who has been there. You are no longer alone.

On this planet, there are many of us who have suffered from mental illness. There are many of us who have suffered from addiction. There are millions of us who have thought about suicide. There are countless more that have lived through the disease of depression. If you have ever listened to the voice of mental illness, it is likely you have heard this voice whisper, "You are worthless. Your life is hopeless...period."

But we can choose to punctuate our life in a different way. With a semicolon.

On a street in Buffalo, I noticed a sign that read something like, "I am not an 'epileptic.'
I am a person with epilepsy." The sign shows something about identity and disease. It is possible for society to label us as a disease, and sometimes we even accept such labels. It is possible for us to identify with our diseases. For many years, I thought of myself as an addict and alcoholic. It is customary in twelve-step circles for us to identify ourselves in this way.

For me, the semicolon is not really an identification with my illness. It is an identification with my recovery; recovery is who I am. I am not ashamed. I am a person who has had mental illness. I am a survivor. My tattoo also means that I am not silent. Despair is a secret that can kill. If you are living with despair and thoughts of suicide, there is help for you. Ask for help. See "Afterword" below for ways to call for help.

Recently, I had a research meeting with my office. We spent the day with visiting professors, planning a grant we were about to submit. After a long and fun day of brainstorming and creation together, we decided to go out to eat. It was a fun group that included my boss, a visiting professor from Australia, and our office research staff. We laughed and shared stories. Everyone ordered a beer or a glass of wine, except me. I ordered a glass of tonic water, as is my habit in these situations. I felt comfortable and happy in the restaurant. As we continued our merriment, the waiter served our drinks. I took a sip of mine and had a complete shock. I felt the numbing effect of alcohol. It was a gin and tonic.

I panicked. I had not had a sip of alcohol for over twenty-three years. I felt the sensation spread through me, from one sip of alcohol. Despite thousands of meetings and thousands of days clean, despite a transformed life in recovery, my perception was altered. My mental illness became active.

Incredibly, my first thought was, *Nobody at the table knows this is a gin and tonic.* My boss and another staff member knew I was in recovery. But they hadn't caught on that the waiter had served alcohol to me. My thoughts raced ahead, *You can drink the whole thing, and no one will know! DRINK IT! DRINK IT!*

I admit I was shocked to find that, after twenty-two years, I still liked the feeling of alcohol. After all the heartache, and all the loss, and all the pain, I still had the same little voice inside me, telling me to go back. But this is the core of addiction and is also the heart of mental illness. And it is something that no longer hides in my unexplored room.

I quietly signaled the waiter and told him what had happened, and I think he read the panic on my face. He quickly took the gin away and brought me a fresh glass of plain tonic water. I drank three more glasses of water with dinner. I still reeled with the discovery that, despite all these years of recovery, my disease was alive and well.

And then I looked down at my left wrist.
On the inside of my wrist, facing me, where no one else could see, was a tattoo.
I remembered the end of my sentence, and I remembered how I had kept writing.

The embarrassing hidden taboo,
    this mental illness,
        concealed away in my unexplored room, has become some-
        thing external.

Taboo has become my tattoo.

꼭

Reflection

Create a quiet moment in a quiet place. Sit comfortably with your feet on the floor and your back straight, if you can. Breathe in deeply, and then breathe out deeply. Do this again and notice your body beginning to relax.

As you move into this relaxed state, what does your heart know about your own story? Has depression hidden in your unexplored room? Is there anxiety? Unresolved grief? Trauma? Family-of-origin wounds?
Are there addictive patterns of behavior that have kept you stuck?

Take another deep breath and drop further into your heart.
It takes great courage to admit we own something forbidden.

If a taboo lives inside us, it takes a strong heart to ask for help.
But to remain silent is to stay stuck.
You do not have to bear this any longer.

What does your heart desire?
What does your heart know now?

When we face taboo in our unexplored room, at first we feel isolated and alone...as if we are the only ones who struggle with this.
This is only an illusion...
We are not alone.

Can you break silence? Can you break taboo?
Are you ready to open your heart to someone?

Breathe in deeply, and then exhale fully. Let this sink in more deeply into your being.

Open your eyes when you are ready to come back to the room where you are sitting.

Chapter Ten
In the Backseat

How much of my mother has my mother left in me?
How much of my love will be
insane to some degree?
And what about this feeling that
I'm never good enough?
Will it wash out in the water, or
is it always in the blood?

—JOHN MAYER

In Steven Spielberg's movie *A.I. Artificial Intelligence*, the young-appearing Haley Joel Osment plays David, a realistic little boy. David is really an android, who has been programmed with the possibility of displaying (and feeling) an emotional bond with his mother. Although his adoptive mother is initially ambivalent about David, she eventually activates the internal imprinting protocol. The protocol creates inside David an unbreakable childlike attachment to her.

David's biological brother becomes jealous of their mother's attention, and eventually he creates a crisis that makes David appear dangerous in the family swimming pool at a party. David's mother is embarrassed and worried. She is not bonded to David in the way he is bonded to her, and she decides to get rid of him. She drives David out into a remote wooded area and leaves him on the roadside, like a stray dog, to fend for himself. Here David's quest to survive begins, as he passes through many dangers.

Central to David's journey is the theme of one-way attachment between him and his mother. David imagines that if he can somehow become a "real boy" like his biological brother, then he can regain his mother's love. The drive to regain his mother's love powers his journey. Ultimately, in this science-fiction tale, David is suspended in sleep for thousands of years, outlasting his parents and outlasting the entire human species.

In a new era, he is awakened by advanced androids. His first waking thought is of his mother. His central desire is to somehow regain her love, and as the movie closes, the advanced androids of the future use a fragment of her hair and his memories to recreate David's mother and his childhood home. The illusion only lasts for twenty-four hours, but that is enough. David and his mother spend a magical day together, as his ultimate wish fulfillment.

This story draws our attention to a longing for attachment that does not fade, even after several thousand years. And if we look honestly within our unexplored rooms, we may find longings for heart connections that are surprisingly durable.

In the film *Thanks for Sharing*," the Tim Robbins character quips, "Feelings are like children." He explains to his twelve-step sponsee, "You don't want them driving the car, but you don't want to stuff them in the trunk either."

Emotions, like children, do not have the capacity to understand or to reason in an abstract sense. They are simple, childlike energies that pass judgment on the current moment. They are sitting in the back seat. And they always want to drive the car.

Even though it is hard to be objective in the moment, there is much that can be learned by observing what goes on behind us in the back seat.

There is a Zen teaching that human beings actually have seven senses, not five. In addition to the traditional five senses of touch, taste, smell, vision, and hearing, there are two more. Emotions and thoughts are added as the sixth and seven senses. These two senses are sources of information, too, much like touch and sight.

If a random surprising thought interrupts us, it is possible for us to stop and notice it for a minute. We can ask ourselves, "What might be going on here? Why am I thinking about this?"

If a situation triggers us, and a strong feeling flares up, it is possible to pause and notice our emotion with a little curiosity. We can turn around and pay attention to the kids in the back seat. We can acknowledge them. It is possible for us to turn around and say, "Hello, I see you. And no, you can't drive the car right now."

Sometimes, it is helpful to honor our back-seat voices. In Ralph Helmick's powerful sculpture, the blues musician Stevie Ray Vaughan stands upright, holding his guitar at his side, like a staff. But the bronze sculpture in Austin also shows another side of Stevie. Behind Stevie's upright figure stretches a bronze shadow of his image, flat on the ground. And in his bronze shadow from behind, Stevie holds up the guitar and is playing the blues. This image captures a truth about his musicianship.

Stevie's most popular and resonant work came from his unexplored room. When Stevie found recovery from drugs and alcohol back in 1986, he wrote about his journey in recovery and created the Grammy-winning album *In Step*. These songs channeled emotions from the back seat. Stevie Ray played guitar and sang from his shadow.

Another example of honoring our emotions in the back seat is found in the recent Pixar movie *Inside Out*. In this groundbreaking film, we are taken inside the mind of a girl named Riley from Minnesota, and we learn that there are five personalities inside of her. Her core emotions are like people: Joy, Sadness, Disgust, Fear, and Anger. These five personalities live together in a high-rise building called "Riley's Headquarters." Although Joy is initially in charge of Headquarters, this begins to change.

When Riley's family relocates to San Francisco for her father's new job, Riley becomes lonely and disconnected from her old friends. Joy is no longer in charge of Headquarters. The internal personalities of Anger, Disgust, and Fear take over, prompting Riley to run away from home, with the intent of returning to Minnesota. Her life is in crisis.

Eventually, Riley listens to her Sadness. When she is able to do this, she sees her life in a new context. When she allows Sadness to take control of Headquarters, her life begins to change for the better. She returns home and tearfully shares her inner struggle and loneliness with her parents. A powerful central theme of Riley's story is that our sadness can orient us. Our sadness is precious. Sometimes, being conscious of sadness can help us to reconstruct our life.

Within all twelve-step traditions is a teaching that another kind of emotion will predictably result in relapse. It is the sustained, perpetuated anger of resentment, and I have experienced the truth of this teaching. There is a strong incentive for us to pay close attention to anger when it surfaces, if we want to recover. This is why, in the language of AA, we are told we must deal with our resentments by cleaning up our side of the street. For resentment, we have to look at our part of a conflict and look at how we may have contributed to the thing we resent. Ultimately, we are coached to "accept the things that we cannot change, and to change the things that we can."

Another way of looking at anger comes from the Zen tradition. In Japan, the Zen tradition, which influenced Samurai, was called "the way of the warrior," or *Bushido*. The warrior's sword was handled with spiritual consciousness. It was taught that the angry warrior would always die.

In Zen, beneath anger we always find the fear of loss, and beneath our fear, we may even find sadness. Our emotions provide critical information that becomes available when we quietly sit with them. Our quest is not to suppress anger, but to understand it. We face our fear and sadness. David Deida remarks, "A fearful man who knows he is fearful is far more trustable than a fearful man who isn't aware of his fear."

I think that both the twelve-step and Zen traditions have it right. It is important for us to own and release our resentments. But it is also important to own the fear and loss that lie beneath our anger.

If certain emotions were unacceptable when we were little, then we stored this material away in our unexplored room. In my house, anger was believed to be a sinful thing, and I was not permitted to be angry when I was young. For others, loss, sadness, and tears were unacceptable growing up.

"Boys don't cry," we were told. Sometimes, any expression of fear was not allowed. "Don't be afraid!" we were admonished.

Whenever portions of our emotional repertoire were not permitted, then they are invisible to us, until they take command of the back seat in adulthood. Author Alice Miller says, "A child can experience her feelings, only when there is somebody there who accepts her fully, understands her, and supports her." If it is not safe for us to show our emotions in childhood, then they are hidden beneath the surface.

If our emotions have been suppressed and we look into our back seat to recognize them riding behind us, then we have finally re-entered our unexplored room to find something stored there long ago. This is where our personal work waits for us.

Debbie Ford notes that "perfect love" is to feeling what "perfect white" is to color. Many think white is the absence of color. It is not. It is the inclusion of *all* color—white is every other color that exists combined. Love is the sum of all emotion (tenderness, hatred, anger, passion, lust, jealousy, generosity, envy, and compassion). Authentic heart connection is built out of all our emotions, even the ones we hide.

As you might guess, one emotion that has ridden in my back seat is anger. I ordinarily don't express my anger publicly, but I have certainly heard it beating on the seat behind me for my attention. There are times when Suzi will, with good intention, pester me about spending too much time on the computer or about something around the house I said I would do but haven't done yet. If I am triggered by her words, then I might say hello to an anger that is out of proportion to whatever is going on in the moment.

Anger also has come up for me if I am triggered in our sexual space, as a couple. I might ask Suzi if she wants to have sex, and she might reply no, or "not tonight." If we have made plans earlier to make love, and she has changed our plans unexpectedly, I might be triggered. If I am triggered, I feel anger, but when I sit with it, underneath my anger is sadness that is totally out of proportion to the moment.

Suzi once told me that when it comes to sex, I can be like Oliver Twist, when he asks, "Please, sir. May I have some more?" I was struck by the truth of her observation, and it is something I have worked on in my men's group. In moments like these, instead of showing up as a man in the bedroom with passion who has something to give, I have shown up as a little boy with unmet dependency needs.

My thirteen-year-old self can be both angry and sad with his unmet needs. He does not want me to wait for pleasure. He is not very big on citizenship in the home, either. He particularly does not want me to help cook or clean. He wants to have sex, escape, and eat ice cream. From the back seat, he clamors, "Let's run away from here!"

My stirred-up, angry thirteen-year-old always wants to drive the car.

When I first started doing this work, I looked back at my passenger with a little curiosity and asked, "What was really going on when I was thirteen?" Then it began to come back to me.

When I was thirteen, the first signs of my attachment issues had surfaced. I unconsciously began to feel some of the anger from unmet needs around my adoption. Like many adopted kids, I blamed my mom for an injury she had nothing to do with. Underneath my anger was actually a sadness and a loss.

I was also enmeshed with my mom, who was perfectionistic and controlling, and our relationship was deteriorating when I was thirteen. My dad traveled often. It felt to me as if mom was overinvested in and hypercritical of me. She picked out my clothes every day and kept close management over the length of my hair. When I verbally defied her as a rebellious teenager, she became enraged. She told me I was incorrigible. She told me she wished she had never adopted me. I felt worthless.

Mom, Dad, and I had issues around sex, too. I found copies of my dad's *Playboy* magazines and was caught hiding them under my bed. This led to a confrontation between us, where I was shamed for looking at his erotica. She also shamed me about masturbation on several occasions and threatened to tie my hands to the bed. I grew to be ashamed of my sexuality.

When I was thirteen, I experimented with drugs. Not too long afterward, I ran away from home and was found by the police a few days later. I was kicked out of the eighth grade. My behavior at thirteen was a public embarrassment to her in our community. After that, she repeatedly told me I had ruined her chance of happiness in life.

Greg Loewen

Of course my thirteen-year-old was pissed. And sad. And afraid.

As the year progressed, it seemed to me I might be discarded soon. My mother talked about sending me to "boys' camp." I was terrified. When I turned fourteen, I transformed into a model student. I was bright, and compliance propelled me forward. By age nineteen, I was accepted into medical school, and I married and moved away from home. My adolescent anger was thrust deep into my unexplored room.

In the years that passed, like David in *A.I.*, on some level, I still longed for a heart connection with my mother. We made a superficial peace as adults, even though I never completely earned her acceptance or trust. Mom moved in with us during her final years, as her dementia deepened. When Mom died, my dad shocked me with something extremely personal I could not even comprehend.

As my mom's life drew to a close on hospice, my dad confided something unimaginable. With some sadness, he told me that the two of them, in their sixty-four years of marriage, had never had sex. He told me he was never physically able to be sexual with her.

I am not able to ask my beloved parents for their permission to tell this story, and I have carefully weighed my disclosure about this part of their lives. As I have sat with it, I have become clear that their story is part of my story, too. Intimate dysfunction between parents affects the entire family. Although their sexual abstinence might be unusual, I think any brokenness between partners easily spills out and creates unintended stress within the family system. My wife's therapist once remarked that 96 percent of all families are dysfunctional, and the other 4 percent are in denial. I share my dad's disclosure respectfully, with compassion for both my parents. I share this as a way of showing what my own personal work has looked like.

My thirteen-year-old self's emotions began to come into focus after my dad's revelation. There was never any element of sexual abuse between my mom and me, but I began to see how her unmet sexual energy affected our relationship. Being in a sexless marriage was an injury she had silently lived with. Her intrusion and disapproval of my sexuality as a boy (and later as a young man) now made a little more sense. My thirteen-year-old had lived with enmeshment. No wonder the anger.

Enmeshment with a parent is sometimes called "emotional incest." This is a subtle wound that only surfaces with careful work. Enmeshment in previous eras (either as a "mama's boy" or a "daddy's girl"), was once considered to be a variation of normal. Child labor and large families were accepted as an essential practice that enabled the survival of family groups. In our own generation, this ethos has changed. We have become conscious of how parental behavior handed down to us from previous generations can create unintended trauma.

In my day, I parented the best I could do at the time. So did my parents. If our children continue on this pathway, they, too, will surely identify ways in which we as their parents caused unintentional harm. The term *incest* is so inflammatory in our culture that I felt resistance when I first used it. But this is not an indictment of my parents or anyone else's. "Emotional incest" is an expression that shows how harmful unhealthy parental enmeshment can be.

It is now widely understood that emotional incest happens when parents use their child to meet their own emotional needs. Inside this behavior is a blindness to the natural power gradient between an adult and a child. The child needs the parent and is powerless to refuse the invitation to be a covert partner. Consent is not possible.

The typical scenario for enmeshment is created when there is a parent who is unfulfilled in the adult relationship with their partner. This void may be the result of death or divorce, or merely may be a result of marital dysfunction. Whatever the cause, the normal, healthy emotional exchange between adult partners is not present.

When such a void exists between the partners, one adult will become lonely, angry, or depressed. When there are multiple children, this parent often designates one child as his or her favorite. The parent may even prefer the company of this child over other adults. The parent may confide in the child as if confiding in another adult and extract inappropriate emotional support from the child. The parent's emotional life depends upon how the child shows up.

There is a loss of appropriate boundaries. Sometimes, the parent becomes overly aware of the child's sexuality and violates privacy. The parent also may become overinvolved in every aspect of the child's life, seeking emotional gain through the child's appearance or successes. Their relationship functions as an ego projection: "See what a great parent I am!"

Another version of enmeshment plays out when a parent becomes overly critical and uses guilt as a weapon, as was the case in my life. Children may be treated as friends, dates, or scapegoats, but Pat

Love writes in *The Emotional Incest Syndrome* that the effects are always the same: "The parent is using the child to satisfy needs that should be satisfied by other adults."

For adult children of emotional incest, there are many consequences that have been identified downstream of their abuse. Adult survivors of this behavior often struggle with feeling both privileged and victimized or feeling talented and worthless at the same time. Often, they have endured jealous abuse of the other parent, or a sibling, or a stepparent. Those adult children typically grow up with a sense of guilt, chronic anxiety, or a lack of self-confidence. Sexual problems and romantic relationship problems are also common.

My understanding of emotional incest grew as I did my work in the years following my mom's death. Like Riley, I listened to sadness that was beneath the anger. In a way, I think my angry thirteen-year-old still longed for reconciliation with his mother, just like David, the android boy. The universe provided an opportunity for me.

I went on a retreat to work in my unexplored room again and had the chance to find reconciliation with my mom, years after her death. This was within the context of an exercise called "the tombstone process." But it wasn't about a trip to the cemetery.

The name of the exercise comes from a kind of unconscious behavior known to therapists. Sometimes we have a feeling or a behavior that is difficult to let go of. We may be determined to let go of this dynamic, but then it comes back again. When a dynamic like this keeps coming back, it is usually because it holds some kind of deeper meaning for us. Sometimes, our way of behaving, like shyness, or fear, or anger, can even be a kind of memorial we hold for someone we have loved and lost. It is a tombstone. It is a way of staying connected to the one we have lost.

In my tombstone exercise, soft music played in the dim light. I used my ski coat, a pillow, and a shimmering gold sheet to create a shape that represented my mom, lying on the floor. As she lay there, I was instructed to imagine holding her hand, as I began to talk to her.

I told mom that what I had always wanted from her was nurturing and acceptance. I told her I would never be able to be what she expected me to be. I told her it wasn't my fault she was hurt so badly. It wasn't my fault her life was so difficult. I loved her, but I couldn't fix her.

I was then coached to tell my mom what it was like for me to carry this anger. I told her I carried this anger as a way to stay connected with her. I admitted to her that I carried this anger because I still loved her.

Then we switched places.

I was coached to try to lie down and become my own mom, under the golden blanket. I was to try to imagine looking up at myself. I imagined myself, Greg the grown man, looking down at me. In my mom's identity, I told Greg I loved him. I found myself telling Greg I would never be able to give him what he really needed. But I loved him. I released him, to be free. I told Greg he could let go of his anger.

The music played on. I wept. We switched places one last time.

I pulled a shimmering royal-blue robe around my own shoulders and stood over my mother in a gentle shift of power. I thanked her for the help she had been able to give me. I blessed her. I saw that she had loved me, but she could never give me what I had missed out on as an adopted kid. I loved her, too, and could never give her what she had missed out on in her marriage. I released her, with gratitude. I released my anger.

In this exercise, my anger was pictured as an object I held on to, as an attempt to stay connected to my mom. I was then invited to imagine other ways to stay connected with her. I answered that I would like to remain connected to my mom by remembering her kindness to me, before our difficult passages together when I was thirteen.
Love became her new tombstone.

Sometimes, if we work on our stuff, we encounter people who have done a kind of work around previous conflicts like mine, or around old abuse they once experienced. Their work might have been compelling and wonderful, yet a year later, they find they need to revisit the same issues again. This was true for me. Even with the closure I felt from the tombstone exercise, I have had to revisit my work with Mom at other retreats and at our men's group at home. Why is this?

As human beings, we tend to hold on to our parents, even if they have been frankly abusive because we needed something from them. Therapists call this "unmet dependency needs." If our basic needs were unmet, we would rather hear, "You are not good enough," than hear nothing at all. Even in a relationship that is short on affirmation and nurturing, there is still human connection. Like

David in *A.I.*, we always hope to get what we need, oblivious to the fact that the one to whom we are bonded can never supply us with what we are missing. When unmet dependency love is present, it contains injury for us. In order to grow and heal, we must eventually release it.

The path to recovery from things like parental enmeshment is complex and involves more than a single exercise. There is a growing awareness among therapists of how these injuries heal. It is totally possible for us to recover. Recovery begins as we become comfortable saying, "No. This is not acceptable. This is a boundary I set between us."

Recovery means that we gain a sense of our value and individuality. In science, we talk about how under the microscope, a cell can lose part of its cellular wall. When this happens, we say that the cell has "lost its integrity." Things that were once on the inside of the cell leak into the outside environment. Toxic things that belonged outside the cell walls are able to enter if the cell loses its integrity. Recovery is about repairing healthy walls and reclaiming our integrity.

Healing means that we reshape unhealthy relationships from our past and set new boundaries. The result of doing this work is that our old emotional triggers begin to fade. Visitors from the basement stop coming upstairs. Angry thirteen-year-olds in the back seat quiet down.

If you have ever wondered about your own childhood, I invite you to consider your younger self with gentleness. There are many burdens that we all silently carry. We carry them out of love, but they are still burdens. It is possible to carry love painfully, even when it is a dynamic like anger. But it is also possible for us to look at our pain with honesty and release it.

I would add that for you to read about this kind of work and to think about your own material is a measure of personal bravery. Many cannot do this. It is not uncommon for people to change the subject when someone talks about this stuff. It can be a little uncomfortable. I know I am diving deeper in this book than most of us would normally go. But it is the personal vulnerability of others that has helped me the most in my life, and my highest desire is to pass this on. So thank you for hanging in there. You can do this work too. If you are reading this, it might be because your soul wants to go there, even if it hurts.

Concealed within all our undiscovered rooms is emotional material that manifests like a noisy child in the back seat. Our child carries on and grows louder in order to gain our attention. This is an invitation to do our work and to heal.

Work in the unexplored room is what frees us to navigate without backseat interference.

Reflection

Create a quiet moment in a quiet place. Sit comfortably with your feet on the floor and your back straight, if you can. Breathe in deeply, and then breathe out deeply. Do this again until you notice your body beginning to relax.

Within your deep relaxation, enter your unexplored room with curiosity.
With your mind quiet, did any moments from your childhood float up to the surface?
Are you aware of any feelings tied to these memories?

Do the normal events of life sometimes overwhelm you?
Do you experience recurrent sadness, anger, or fear that gets in your way?

Sadness...
　　Anger...
　　　　Fear...
Were these emotions permitted to surface within your family structure?

Did you have a parent who was unable to meet your needs
　　or who was unable to love you with neutral generosity?

Did you struggle with a parent who was enmeshed with you?

Is this part of your struggle today?

Do you have childhood emotions that sometimes try to drive your adult car?

If you allow yourself to look at your family's dysfunction,
you have not betrayed your family system.
Instead, you perform an act of kindness for the little one inside of you,
who was afraid, hurt, and angry.

What does your heart know about what that little one needs?

Breathe in deeply, and then exhale fully. Open your eyes when you are ready to come back to the room where you are sitting.

Chapter Eleven
Synchronicity

I saw the sign, and it opened up my eyes,
I saw the sign.

—Jonas Berggren

There was once a brilliant, young neuropsychiatrist who studied under Sigmund Freud in Vienna. The young doctor specialized in suicide and developed a legendary and successful suicide program in Vienna's psychiatric hospital. In 1938, when the unification of Austria and Nazi Germany was nearly complete, he was stripped of his title as a physician and forced to resign from the hospital, because he was Jewish. He continued to practice as a "specialist" at a Jewish hospital. In 1942, he married and managed to procure a visa for himself and his new wife, so they could escape to the United States. He went home to talk to his father about their plans.

At his father's house, he noticed a small slab of marble with a single Hebrew inscription. He asked his father about it. His father explained that the synagogue had been detonated, and from the rubble, he had salvaged a fragment of the Ten Commandments.

The young man asked him which commandment it was. His father answered that it was the fifth commandment: "Honor your father and your mother."

The young psychiatrist was deeply touched by the meaning of this marble fragment and canceled his plans to escape to the United States.

This was a decision that would turn the course of Dr. Viktor Frankl's life upside down. Within a few months, he, his mother, father, sister, and wife would all be deported by train to concentration camps at the hands of the Nazis. His mother, father, and wife would perish. The young psychiatrist eventually would find himself imprisoned at Auschwitz. It was within the confines of a death camp that his most beautiful and profound observations of the human interior would occur.

In Auschwitz, Frankl found himself working in the field of psychiatry again, counseling his fellow prisoners. One day, a young prisoner confided that he had been struggling with the idea of suicide. The young man told Frankl he could no longer expect anything from life. Frankl surprised himself with an unrehearsed question: "Ask yourself then, if you can no longer expect anything from life, what is it that life is expecting from you?"

As Frankl tried to comfort and encourage his fellow prisoners, he also started to notice what life was expecting from him. It was something internal that kept him from giving up. Frankl found that the memory of his wife sustained him, even though he had no way of knowing whether she was still alive. Her memory was what contained deep meaning for him. His work was another.

Frankl also noticed that when his fellow prisoners lost their sense of meaning, they gradually collapsed into despair and apathy. When this happened, their self-care disappeared, and they would walk around the camp almost like zombies. It was an ominous event, because any self-neglect promptly turned to death in the harsh environment. It became increasingly clear that there was one thing that conferred survival on human beings who lived in such peril: their personal sense of meaning. It was possible to survive great suffering, if one was able to hold on to a sense of meaning.

After his release from the death camp, Frankl wrote the words no one yet has ever been able to successfully challenge: "Life is never made unbearable by circumstances, but only by lack of meaning and purpose."

In 1946, his experience became the beloved spiritual classic known as *Man's Search for Meaning*. His book has been translated into twenty-four languages and has sold over ten million copies.

During my active addiction, I found myself living in a universe that often seemed meaningless, hostile, and random. When I was in this passage, I lived with a constant low-grade current of fear and despair. It was only relieved with substance use.

When I entered recovery, I began to entertain the notion that my world might not be as hostile as I had thought. I would walk into an AA meeting, sit at a table, and find that the topic was exactly what I had been struggling with. I would drive down a random street in some kind of crisis, only to spot an AA friend, who would pile into my car and help me through the crisis. Over and over, coincidences piled up. Something was saving my life. The universe did not seem very random any longer. The maxim I learned in the AA tradition was that "Coincidence is God's way of being anonymous."

Carl Jung taught that recognizing meaningful coincidences was a key for spiritual growth. One of Jung's favorite stories came from Lewis Carroll's *Through the Looking Glass and What Alice Found There*. In this scene, the White Queen offers Alice a job and tells her about the terms of employment: "Two pence a week, and jam every other day."

But then the queen clarifies the matter of the every-other-day jam for Alice: "The rule is: jam tomorrow, and jam yesterday, but never jam today."

Alice objects. It seems to her that there must be a time when jam comes today.

The queen replies that if Alice can only "remember things that have happened in the future," then she will be able to say that jam came today.

For Jung, this story was a way of explaining what happens when we notice a coincidence. A coincidence is like déjà vu. If we only could remember the future, then we would sense that we had been here before. Just as the White Queen proposed, we would recognize why something is happening, even before it actually happens.

Imagine standing before a giant measuring tape, marked in years. It is a time line. In fact, it is *your* time line. It stretches back to the day of your birth and stretches forward to the day of your death. Find today, the present moment. Stand at this point. From this point, look backward and try to remember something that has happened to you. Now, turn and look forward on the time line, toward the future. Remember anything?

If we think of coincidence as a kind of déjà vu, then we have been here before. We have opened a pathway that connects the past with the future. Coincidence becomes an event that is pregnant with significance. Jung held that "meaningful coincidences" unveil something unseen about how life works, and he coined the term *synchronicity* for this powerful phenomenon. Synchronicity means that life is not a series of random events. Instead, coincidences are an expression of a deeper order.

In our century, connectedness has become a kind of reality to physicists who study subatomic particles. There is a deeper order to the subatomic world that resembles the part of the world that is visible to us in daily life. In his spiritual classic *The Tao of Physics*, physicist Fritjof Capra notes, "Even though two electrons are far apart in space, they are nonetheless linked by instantaneous nonlocal connections…the universe is fundamentally interdependent, interconnected and inseparable." This is the deeper order that Jung saw.

In my younger life, when I was surprised by something good, I dismissed it as serendipity: It was merely a random good thing. But unlike synchronicity, serendipity contains no irony.

Although synchronicity is meaningful, it is not always pleasant. And when bad things happen, we often notice a desire within ourselves to find a deeper order, even if we do not really believe in the deeper order. We naturally tend to look for the outline of a face in the image of the moon. It has been my experience that we usually try to find patterns in the life events that come to us.

In my career as a physician, there have been countless times when it was my duty to break bad news to a patient and his or her family. The news was often the diagnosis of cancer. When a devastating diagnosis and the inevitability of death sinks in, I have found that the most common question that people ask me is, "Why? Why is this happening to me?"

A therapist might gently ask, "Why not you?"
I have always felt this question is not for me to answer as a physician. This is a question that comes from the deepest corner of our unexplored room. The answer to questions like this can only be found where we store a special map—our map of what our world is really like.

This little map develops in childhood through the actions of the adults who have cared for us. Our map might contain religious images and belief structures, if these have been taught to us. But our map has really formed from how we experienced emotional security. It is a map we may forget about as we grow older, but it remains in our unexplored room and is part of our certainty. The map is not what we tell everyone about what we believe. It is what we secretly tell ourselves.

It is what we tell ourselves in a crisis.
The answer to the question "Why did this happen to me?" is found here.

We often revise this map as we work on our stuff. M. Scott Peck says that "psychotherapy is, among other things, a process of map-revising." So are the experiential workshops that are the central part of my own story, told in this book. Our map revision depends on the experiences we have had. Sometimes, these are experiences we can actually choose to have as a part of our personal work. Our map revisions show our coincidences and show how we have been loved.

Once, in a workshop for personal work, I was asked to pick a man to play the childhood part of myself, at nine months. I chose an aging, balding southern man from our group. He had blue eyes and a gentle presence. He sat in a chair before me, representing young Greg. The facilitator asked me to look into this man's eyes and see my childhood self.
He asked me what my nine-month-old self really wanted to hear.

I looked in his eyes.
I found myself telling him he was safe.
I told him he was loved.
I told him he needed to experience what he was going through, in order to give away what was in his heart.
As I looked into his eyes, my own eyes grew wet.

I repeated the words, "You are safe. You are loved."
The facilitator produced a small hand mirror. He gently moved it in front of my face.
He asked me to look into my *own* eyes and repeat these affirmations. Through my tears, I repeated that I was loved and that I was safe. As I experienced this message deeply, I began to understand something.

I found myself beginning to smile into the mirror. I could see where my own strength came from. It was from the love that was already inside me.

The facilitator drew me aside after the ritual and asked me to give a word for what this exercise really meant to me. As I reflected on the strength I felt, I could see courage form on my own face when I heard this affirmation. I thought of the word *courage*. My map was changing.

When Suzi and I reunited after thirty years of separation, we had a lot of history to learn from each other. As we started to get re-acquainted, I learned that Suzi had struggled with infertility in her first marriage and had eventually adopted two children. As a mom who loved her adopted kids, she had literally spent decades of her life learning about adoption and the related attachment issues adopted kids may have. She was also a teacher who had specialized in reading and who was trained in brain integration. She was deeply versed in understanding exceptional, brilliant children who process things in atypical ways.

The match between her journey and mine seemed obvious. I happened to be an adopted man who, as an adult, struggled with attachment issues and feelings of abandonment. And I also happened to be a scientist and musician who tended to drive life partners crazy because of my quirky way of processing everyday life. Here was a synchronicity that sparkled!

Reciprocal preparation had landed in my lap over the decades, as I became ready to be Suzi's partner. One of my children suffered from PTSD, secondary to childhood sexual abuse committed by a family acquaintance. For years, my child's struggle was my struggle. We went to therapist after therapist to find healing and understanding.

In addition to this, I was also a physician with training in psychiatry. PTSD and sexual abuse were things I understood and cared about. As we continued to update each other, I learned from Suzi that she had also suffered from PTSD, as a result of sexual abuse that had occurred in her childhood. Another synchronicity for my map.

When I first felt deep attraction to Suzi as a teenager, it was many years before any of these coincidences would manifest. As the White Queen suggested, our teenage attraction could have been like remembering a heart connection before it actually happened. Our future would connect to our past someday. There was meaning in our coincidences.

Of course, long-term relationships may begin as healing partnerships, but if they flourish, they develop other qualities, too. Healing is only a small part of our connection now. But it was very affirming to see how our journey prepared each of us to understand the other's wounds. If there was ever synchronicity, this was it.

Some years ago, an intuitive female counselor suggested I go on a men's retreat held out in the woods. After a year of procrastination, I was finally ready to sign up. I knew no one who had ever done this retreat, so when I received the registration materials, I was taken aback. Their language seemed a little authoritarian, almost militaristic. It was obvious to me that if I did the weekend, I was in for a challenge. I was unsure about whether I should go.

Sometimes, when I am on the edge of a major decision in my life, I will sit in silence and try to find my direction. You might even say that I will attempt to remember the future. If we are conscious of our surroundings, anything will work for this purpose. We might get a sense of what we should do when we see the shape of a cloud, notice a random phrase from an overheard conversation, or notice a bird or animal when we go for a walk. Anything we find can hold significance that will help us to get in touch with our internal truth.

Sometimes when I am trying to sort out what is true for me in this way, I will hold pictured cards with intention and will then look with openness to see what turns up.

I have a deck of "Ascended Masters" cards created by Doreen Virtue, and in this deck, the Masters are spiritually enlightened beings from a broad spectrum of traditions (e.g., Moses, Buddha, Manjushri, Saint Germaine, and Yoganandya). As I sat with my workshop-registration materials, I held the cards with intention and considered my question: "Should I go on this retreat?"

I randomly drew one card. On the face of the card was the image of "The Green Man."

The picture on this card was a mysterious, leafy forest man, dressed in green. Back then, I was completely unfamiliar with the green man mythology, and I had to look it up. The Green Man is found throughout the world and is a particularly commonly carved figure in the ancient cathedrals of Europe. The Green Man has been recently taken to represent nature and ecology, but he has always been a symbol of personal growth and transformation.

My card seemed to say to me at that moment, "Your destiny is in the woods."
I took this as my answer and decided to register for the weekend retreat.

The retreat changed my life. At a final ceremony during the weekend, something remarkable happened. I was part of a giant circle of perhaps a hundred participants, and we sat together in the firelight. As I turned, I saw a figure approach me from behind. It was a staff member from the retreat, whose face, arms, and legs were completely painted with green pigment. He was covered with leaves. He was dressed to represent the Green Man.

The Green Man came behind me, placed his hand on my back, and whispered into my ear, "Remember..."

And of course I remembered. I remembered holding the card of the Green Man in my deck a few weeks before. Synchronicity. This was a secret that I kept for years.

But it did not end there. About eight years later, my wife attended a women's retreat in Glastonbury. As she prepared to return home, she wanted to find a present for me to thank me for my support of her work. She did not know about my work or the card I had drawn years before. Using her intuition, she found a necklace with a pendant for me. It was the Green Man, once again. The Green Man was something I remembered from my future. Synchronicity happened to us again.

Synchronicity is an affirmation. My mentor teaches that synchronicity is one of the final events in any creative process. Creation starts when we allow a desire to surface. We picture our desire, and then place ourselves in the picture. We fall in love with the picture we have created. The picture gains definition as we play with it. Our next step is to create physical anchors for our creation as we build it in real time. If our creation comes from our hearts, then this is the moment when meaningful coincidences start to pop up everywhere. I have experienced the truth of this many times.

A few years ago, I felt a desire to begin to write about my own healing process and how shadow work in its various forms propelled my personal growth. I was interested in how such work might affect our ability to deliver health care, among other things. Every time I conversed about my experience of heart connection in the practice of medicine, I felt energized. My desire came from my heart. I pictured myself working and writing about this and fell in love with my picture. I met with my mentor after creating six chapters of the book you are now reading. Physical anchors for my creation were forming. My mentor encouraged me to continue, and I had no idea of what to expect. It was time for meaningful coincidence.

A few months later, I received a curious e-mail from someone named Gregory V. Loewen. Gregory V. Loewen had found my name on the Internet when he was Googling himself. He learned that Gregory M. Loewen is a nationally known physician scientist with dozens of scientific publications. When I looked up Gregory V. Loewen, I found that he is an internationally known sociologist philosopher, author of over twenty books, and chairman of his department in a major Canadian University.

Gregory V. posed a surprising question in his introductory e-mail to me. He asked me if he could interview me for a book he was writing. His book was on the subject of the philosophy of health care. I fell off my seat. Of course I would be delighted to do the interview!

Greg Loewen

I considered his thoughtful interview questions and returned five pages of replies. One thing had become clear. We had to talk. And talk we did, for hours on Skype. As we now do every month. Not only did I acquire a new friend (who is probably a distant relative), but I also have acquired a new writing partner. We are now working on a book together about the philosophy of health care.

My experience led me to think more about how we create synchronicity in our lives. Something called "the Law of Attraction" ties to an often-repeated phrase that declares, "Like attracts like." This idea has been popularized in many venues, including the 2006 movie *The Secret.* "Like attracts like" promotes the notion that, if we focus on negative ideas like poor health, dysfunctional relationships, or scarcity, then we will attract negative events like illness, broken relationships, and poverty. Conversely, if we focus on the positive, the law of attraction predicts that we will attract positive outcomes like good health, happy relationships, and wealth. This idea contains similarities to the prosperity gospel of some modern Christian churches.

Skeptics argue that there is no scientific evidence for such a law, but I think there might be a partial truth here. As a physician, I can certainly see how negative thinking can translate into depression and poor health, and this is a well-supported observation in science. I have even seen similar patterns in my own life experience.

But there is a problem. If like really only attracts like, then we should legitimately expect wealth, happy relationships, and good health, if we only put our minds to it. But experience teaches us that life is more complicated than this. Sometimes we are positive and do our parts, only to be met with disaster. As a therapist, it is also easy to think of circumstances where someone will divorce his or her abusive partner, only to attract another abusive partner. Perhaps like does not always attract like. Perhaps sometimes we attract a lesson. Synchronicity is not simple.

If the law of attraction is absolute, then how could Frankl attract such unspeakable suffering? Surely he thought positive things. One uncomfortable implication of any Law of Attraction is a naïve blame of the victim. The law predicts that anyone who experiences a disaster must have attracted it. When we attribute cause and effect like this, we are back at our map, imagining simple connections between the events in our lives. Straight lines of blame might give us a sense of power or safety. But as we grow older, our map inevitably grows larger and more complex. The straight lines between cause and effect have become more curved, or even indistinct. With such a larger, more realistic map, we learn to sit with a sense of openness when something bad happens. Wisdom teaches us to be comfortable with mystery.

Synchronicity eventually seemed to take form in Frankl's life, and he found a deeper order to his journey. Jung might even suggest that synchronicity could be found in the slab of marble recovered from the synagogue. It seems clear that Frankl's response to suffering provided all of us with a courageous insight that lives on, long after his death. There is a strong, invisible connection between Carl Jung and Victor Frankl, because synchronicity and meaning are related.

Synchronicity is dizzying, Alice once observed. But it is a dizzy, powerful affirmation of a deeper reality. I couldn't make this up.

Reflection

Create a quiet moment in a quiet place. Sit comfortably with your feet on the floor and your back straight, if you can. Breathe in deeply, and then breathe out deeply. Do this again until you notice your body beginning to relax.

As your body relaxes, allow memories from your life to filter up to your consciousness. With neutrality and curiosity,
notice if there are any events from your life
that once seemed difficult, or even painful in the moment.

What happens if you look for synchronicity in your life story?
Could there be a thread of meaning that runs through your life?

Could a difficult passage of your life be a class?
Did it prepare you for something?

Allow your consciousness to drift from the past into the future.
Can you imagine a future that might make sense with your past?

Have you been preparing for an amazing relationship?

Have you been preparing for a special work?

Breathe in a sense of kindness from the earth below you.
Breathe in the sense of support that holds you.

You are sitting with mystery...
You are sitting next to a meaning that remains invisible.

Breathe in deeply, and then exhale fully. Open your eyes when you are ready to come back to the room where you are sitting.

Chapter Twelve
Playing with Death

Oh, I'll be free
just like that bluebird...
Oh, I'll be free
Ain't that just like me?

—DAVID BOWIE

At the end of "Lazarus," David Bowie's final music video, he sings from his death bed. Inside his bedroom rests an armoire with the doors ajar, hinting at the tomb-like darkness that rests next to him. He gets up and gradually backs himself into the darkness of the armoire, and then closes the doors. He sings about being free, as he vanishes. Lazarus goes out with a song.

In the ancient tradition of the Bible story, Lazarus became ill and died. After his body was left in the tomb for four days, Jesus entered the tomb and commanded his friend to "come forth." In the story, Lazarus returned to life and exited the tomb wearing a burial shroud. Lazarus was the first recorded "near-death experience," or NDE, with a death time that lasted a little longer than average.

What happens next, of course, is not detailed in the scriptural account. Nowhere do we find a hint that Lazarus, who was once raised from the dead, is now immortal. It seems to me that it is likely that Lazarus must have grown old. He must have found himself facing death for the second time. But as with any NDE survivor, death would be more familiar to him than to most. Perhaps this is why Bowie's Lazarus plays with death and sings about freedom and bluebirds as he leaves.

Accounts of Bowie's last days suggest he entered the end of life with a similar bravado. His cause of death was reputed to be liver cancer, but no one seems to know for sure, because this was not a subject Bowie shared publicly. With seeming intentionality, it is reported that Bowie spent much of the last weeks of his life working in the recording studio with fellow musicians, making the final touches on what was to be his musical epitaph. Bowie did not seem to spend time dying, because dying was not his identity, unless it was in the ironic jest of his video. He lived life, and then it was over.

It is not uncommon for celebrities to talk about their illnesses publicly, in order to garner charitable support, especially if it is an underappreciated illness or an illness that is considered shameful. Much of the charitable support for cancer and other illness comes from this kind of courage. On the other hand, there is also an idea that identification with illness is not a healthy way to understand ourselves and to move through life. When I read about David Bowie's response to illness, I thought to myself, *Here is someone who was not a "dying man" or a "cancer victim." Instead, here is someone who identifies with life and was informed by death.*

Western medicine is a masculine, left-brained science with a narrow intention to cure disease and prevent death. This intention is powerful, but the unswerving allegiance to this aim can also produce extensive collateral damage. In order to cure, we often cause harm.

As physicians and caregivers, our traditional focus is to save life. We have made a "war on cancer" and fought a "battle against AIDS"; normally, we take no prisoners in our fight against disease. In order to rid the patients of their cancer cells, we also destroy their hair follicles—not to mention the lining of the gut, the bone marrow where new blood cells are grown, and the patients' energy level. At the end of the day, when the battlefield is strewn with casualties, we imagine there is only one victor. The patient survives, and the disease is dead.

In Western medicine, we celebrate survival, both in the scientific literature (as the litmus test of a good treatment) and in real celebrations, such as a "Survivor's Day" at a cancer center. To survive is everything, and to succumb to disease is to fail. In the tradition of scientific cancer literature, death is referred to as "treatment failure."

Celebrations of survival affirm the courage and determination that cancer patients exhibit. They inspire all of us to love life more, to be present, and to fulfill our mission in this world. It is not uncommon for my cancer patients to complete a very difficult series of chemotherapies, radiation treatments, or surgery where they endure pain and difficult side effects in their fight to stay alive.

In my office, I often find myself saying to them, "Thanks for working so hard just to be here." I get it. I tell them this, because in contrast, I am here (sometimes unconsciously) without having to do anything at all.

I feel humbled by their work.

Regarding his own experience of cancer therapy, Roger Ebert once remarked, "Although people in my situation are always praised for their courage, actually courage has nothing to do with it. There is no choice." The choices we make when we are in peril may not seem very heroic to us. But after making this passage with many patients, it is my sense that entering treatment means to choose in the face of fear. And it takes at least as much courage to refuse treatment.

If Lazarus of the Bible eventually faced a terminal illness, he would have been considered a treatment failure by modern medicine. Contemporary physicians would say he had a poor outcome, because survival has been our only measurement of success. Ultimately, all of us are treatment failures.

A new discipline has recently surfaced outside of the curative-intent paradigm of modern medicine. It is called "comfort care" or "palliative care." In the field of palliative care, the intention of caregivers is not to cure; it is to heal. To heal someone in this context does not mean to eradicate disease. To heal means to make whole. Healing is weaving together something that has been torn apart. To palliative medicine, we are more than a physical body with a malady of the moment. If we can help someone integrate his or her life, then he or she will live well and can also die in peace. In this light, the second death would have looked quite differently to Lazarus, because he had already been healed. If healing was the intention, then death was not a failure.

Patients who face death from cancer or other terminal illnesses often find themselves engaged in spiritual transformation as they let go of the things that no longer matter. It is much easier to let go of life and to surrender when our personal work is finished. Although the completion of personal work in our unexplored room seems complicated, it really isn't. Sometimes completion is only to say a few little words that have been unspoken. The ability to find peace and surrender at the end of life may be elusive until these simple messages are given a voice. Such messages create healing inside us, if they are addressed to ones who have heart connections with us.

In his landmark book *Dying Well*, palliative-care physician Ira Byock describes the prescriptions he has written for hospice patients who are struggling with unfinished business. I have written similar prescriptions in my own practice. Sometimes, in order to help patients heal their past, a prescription might read:

- Say "Thank you."
- Say "I'm sorry."
- Say "Please forgive me."
- Say "I forgive you."
- Say "I love you."
- Say "Good-bye."

We do not have to wait until our last breath to do this work. We do not need to wait until terminal illness strikes us before we begin to voice these messages.

In our unexplored room remains one last shrouded personality. Death itself is the feared, tabooed figure who waits for us. But if we ever become acquainted with Death, we may be surprised to find he is like a wise person, who has the capacity to provide us with deep advice about what really matters. Death invites us to do personal work.

When Death becomes our counselor, he invites us to say hello to our heart connections. At the end of life, they are what matter the most. Death tells us to give everything away. We no longer need anything: we are enough. If we have unfinished work within our unexplored room, Death invites us to enter the wound and to heal if we can. Old taboos become meaningless, and the only thing that matters is who we really are. The only thing that matters is the love we have stayed for. Death invites us to look back on our lives and notice synchronicities. There are no coincidences anymore. It was all meant to be.

Death was not something we talked about when I was small. I was given a detailed description of the afterlife by my family's religious tradition, but I was never allowed to go to funerals as a child. Death was something I learned about in my work space as a physician, but I had never encountered it up close. Death was a feared stranger in my unexplored room, until my parents moved in.

When my parents reached their mideighties, mortality had begun to greet them. My mother had advanced dementia, and my dad had advanced Parkinson's disease when they moved in to live with us. We cared for them for three years in our home, and I watched as they slowly let go of the things they loved. My mother died first, on hospice in our home. My dad lived on for another seven months.

My dad had been an athlete, and he had always been proud of his athletic abilities in football, baseball, basketball, and hockey. For this reason, Parkinson's disease was an ironic illness that struck at the core of what he loved most about his life. It took away his physical ability to walk, to stand, and to move. Despite this, he bore his disease with great dignity and did not complain much. He gradually became bedridden, and I sat with him and held his hand and talked with him in the evenings. He had given up all physical activities. At the end, his wife was gone, and his closest friends were also dead. He knew I loved him, but he was ready to let go.

When I flew back to New York to be with my daughter for her college graduation, I had no idea his death was so imminent. He died the next night, and I was heartbroken when I received the call in my hotel room.

Then something happened that would introduce me to that feared, shrouded figure in my unexplored room. I will share my tale with you, conscious of the fact that it is free from scientific content and that my observations are untestable. Although my experiences seemed real, I understand they may represent dreamlike sounds and images that surfaced in my mind as I processed my own grief. But even if this is true, it doesn't matter. The most vital information we can ever receive about death comes from our heart. Our heart knows what the mind cannot grasp.

I had three visitations from my dad after he passed.

On the morning after he died, my daughter and I made our way to Niagara Falls, where we decided to enter the Cave of the Winds. This attraction begins with an elevator ride leading to a tunnel through the rock that opens to the base of the American falls. It was a warm, clear day in May, and the sun was bright. We climbed up the wooden scaffolding, closer and closer to the base of the falls.

As I stood at the base of the falls, I became unconscious of my daughter and the few tourists around me. I was engulfed by billowing white mist luminous from the sunlight. The roar of the water was deafening. I imagined in my very being that I was at my own moment of death. I felt engulfed by powerful love. I felt warmth, safety, and light. This is when I heard my dad's voice, telling me, "This is what it was like!"
I was overwhelmed.

Later that evening, we were given tickets to a concert by Yanni, who was at the hotel where I was staying. We all sat together in the dark at Shea's Performing Arts Center in downtown Buffalo as the black stage was illuminated by twinkling starlight. The first song began with playfulness but grew into majestic joy. In the darkness, my dad's image came to me. He ran and jumped in the darkness; he was laughing and doing basketball layups among the stars. His movement was restored. He was ecstatic.

My dad's third visitation happened on my plane ride home, when I randomly decided to watch the Robert Redford film *The Natural*. Perhaps it was in my dad's honor. Dad had always loved baseball, and I have fond memories of listening to a crackling radio baseball game with him on summer nights when I was a boy.

Although I remembered liking the movie when it first came out, I had forgotten most of the story. In the final scene, slugger Roy Hobbs is at the end of his career. He is staging a comeback and is up to bat, but his special bat is broken. He asks the bat boy to pick another bat for him. With care, the bat boy chooses a bat, and hands it to Hobbs, who steps up to the plate, and hits a home run. He tips his hat to the boy as he runs, and tips his hat to the crowd as he circles third base. As he runs into home, he is surrounded and embraced by teammates and friends.

One last time, I heard my dad's voice: "You did this for me."

I gave Dad support at the end of his life. I picked out his bat, but he is the one who hit the home run. He is the one who ran the bases, and he was the one who was reunited with the ones he loved. I felt his joy. I felt his affirmation.

For me, the three visitations were a vision quest, leaving me with poetic knowledge from my interior. My heart was introduced to Death, who opened a gateway to restoration and reunion.

The afterlife is untestable. The science around near-death experiences is difficult to perform and provides uncertain conclusions. Religions project certainty about this place where science cannot go. Even though there is nothing wrong with religious views of the afterlife, it is possible to be religiously devout, with well-developed beliefs about the afterlife, and still harbor powerful fears of death.

We cannot be informed by death if we are afraid of it. And when the certainty of our own mortality arrives, we find ourselves back in our unexplored room, sitting before the one we have been avoiding.

But there is a way to befriend Death in our unexplored room. There is a heart knowledge described in chapter 1 that tells us when we are loved. The very same heart knowledge can also tell us something about Death. And if we receive this powerful core knowledge, it is stronger than (or can strengthen) any religious teaching. This is a heart knowledge that comes to us when we encounter our own mortality, either from our own peril or from the loss of someone who was close to us. At these moments, we become open to vision quest images from our hearts.

In the early days of my recovery, I had no belief in the divine, but I was desperate to recover. In the twelve-step tradition, it is taught that the price of admission into recovery is to find and honor some kind of a divinity or god. The twelve-step concept of divinity is friendly to all religious beliefs, and God is referred to as "A Higher Power." My first difficult task as a nonbeliever who wanted to survive was to try to find a Higher Power.

My counselor at the treatment center asked me if I had ever noticed how grass grows up out of the cracks in the sidewalk. I said yes. He pointed out that sometimes life springs up, like the grass, where things look impossible. Sometimes, life and goodness flourish when the odds seem to be against them. He told me I didn't need to believe in "god" to recover. He told me if I wanted to recover, I could just believe in the "life force that helped things to grow in difficult places."

This force became my Higher Power. And so it was for many years.

It is not necessary to carry any religious beliefs or teachings in order to have a personal certainty around death. But it might help to be comfortable with the mystery of goodness. Could there be a life force that allows things to grow in difficult places? Could there be an underlying deeper order, as Jung suggested? Could there be meaning to our existence, as Frankl observed?

You are the only one who knows. What does your heart tell you?

If Death becomes a figure of light who is full of love, restoration, and reunion, then Death is our ally. When I did this work, Death became a new adviser at my shoulder. One day, I found myself asking Death questions about my work space: "If I only had seven years to live, should I keep doing this job?"

Death loves to answer questions like these, and the answer in my heart was no. Consciousness of mortality is a powerful tool.

The no I received led me to quit my job a few years ago, and I started working part time at a small asbestos clinic in western Montana. This is where I started this book, which now nears completion. In my new life, I live less than a mile from the location for the film *The Revenant*. Often in the evenings, I will walk by myself on trails through the woods. It was my ridiculous habit on those unaccompanied walks to bring along a large hunting knife. If you have seen the bear attack in the movie, it might make more sense to you. I am a lifelong city dweller who feels somewhat vulnerable to the wild predators which live in the woods, even though my walks bring me solitude and understanding. Underneath my vulnerability is a trace of my own residual fear of death. Even when we do work around our own mortality, our physical bodies still contain the instinct to live, and we have physical fear that helps us survive.

We cannot choose whether we will die, but we can choose what we would like our death to look like. This is an idea I often share with patients when I talk to them about palliative care or hospice. In a recent survey, it was found that it was quite rare for terminally ill physicians to choose to die in the hospital or in the intensive-care unit. This tendency is unlike the general public, and the reason is simple: doctors know the limitations of such care.

When death is imminent, aggressive interventions might extend life for days or weeks, but aggressive medical interventions will not reverse a terminal process. We physicians do not want to spend the last of our days on earth hooked up to tubes, lines, and life-support machines in the hospital. When patients (or their families) choose these interventions at the end of life, it is usually because they don't understand this. They do not appreciate how little our expensive medical interventions really offer. If an alternative is offered in a compassionate way, then it is possible for us to choose to create a good death for ourselves.

There are as many versions of a good death as there are people. Many would choose to die at home if possible, surrounded by their loved ones. Some might choose religious or spiritual elements for their final hours. But on typical hospice or palliative care, it is also a common and widely accepted practice to give sedating drugs like morphine to help dying patients drift into unconsciousness for their final hours. Studies have shown that when patients control their own pain medication, they need less.

Years ago, during my training, when the AIDS epidemic was raging, death from the complications of AIDS was common. I remember taking care of an ex-heroin addict who was dying from AIDS in the county hospital, back in the 1980s. His dying request to me was that we refrain from giving him any morphine or other drugs. He wanted to leave the earth with consciousness. I was touched by his courage and also a little mystified. Back then, it didn't occur to me that I had just witnessed a heroin addict demonstrate an advanced understanding about the end of life.

What my patient really wanted became clearer to me many years later. My mentor referred me to the book *Deathing: An Intelligent Alternative for the Final Moments of Life* by Anya-Foos Graber. In this unique volume, Graber observes that death holds the potential of being a "shining, light-filled conscious moment." She is one who reframed death as a natural event, instead of a disease that should be medicated. She suggests that it is possible for us to prepare for death as one prepares for natural childbirth. She coined the term *deathing* for a partnership between a dying person and a "deathing coach" at the end of life.

Although spiritual coaching at the end of life seems foreign to many, it is accepted in many cultures. We can be coached to identify with the part of us that does not die. In the words of Ram Das, "Death is absolutely safe. It is like taking off a tight shoe. It is release."

Perhaps consciousness is the ultimate way for us to play with death. Consciousness is how we might meet a guide whom we have become unafraid of. When the unexplored room has been opened and illuminated, such a meeting becomes possible. I think perhaps my AIDS patient who refused medications knew this back then.

Greg Loewen

What would it be like to be present with your death? Is it even possible?
What does your heart tell you?

In the Martin Scorsese documentary *Living in the Material World*, George Harrison kept a daily meditation practice for decades. His wife, Olivia, once asked him, "Why do you meditate?"

Harrison replied, "I'm preparing for the hour of my death."

She queried, "So is it working?"

"I don't know yet."

Later, Olivia's tears well up as she describes the incredible scene of her husband's final passage at the end of his life. "If a film crew had been there, no lights would have been needed to shoot the scene."

His practice worked.

What if hospice provided us with a choice for natural death, analogous to the drug-free choice offered for natural childbirth? The opiate-based drugs routinely used at the end of life in hospice culture sedate and dull consciousness in order to relieve anxiety and pain. There is nothing wrong with this, and I have prescribed them many times. We humans must do with what we have. But what if we found natural ways to relieve pain and anxiety instead?

Imagine Lamaze-style classes for breathing techniques and complementary alternative modalities like acupuncture or music for a natural transition; imagine deathing coaches who facilitate spiritual work at the end of life. The honored goal of palliation has always been the *relief of pain*, and this includes even unvoiced discomfort.

What would it be like if *consciousness during transition* was our goal? Maybe this would be a good death for some.

Death work is our eventual task in the unexplored room. Not long ago, I suffered a brainstem TIA, or "transient ischemic attack." This is like experiencing a temporary stroke. A brainstem TIA is a warning sign of a massive, fatal stroke that involves the base of the brain. As I lay on my side on the bedroom floor, I felt calm. Even as the room spun in circles, I was able to tell my wife I loved her and my children. I told her not to allow me to stay on life support if my heart stopped. As I waited, I was conscious of my heart connections. A few minutes later, when my symptoms cleared, I was in the presence of my new guide from my unexplored room.

There is a Native American medicine-wheel teaching about death found in the *Seven Arrows* book written by Hyemeyohsts Storm. On the compass-like medicine wheel, the Mouse energy comes from the direction of the South, which is the place of innocence and trust. The mouse is the one which best perceives what is close at hand.

The Mouse elder teaches his mice, "Never come home wet, with the saliva of your enemy." In other words, it is good to run, and it is good to escape death. But when you are caught in the jaws of the predator, then your journey is over. It is time for you to give yourself up to the universe. Don't try to escape your ending. Surrender, when it is the time for surrender. This is dignity.

There is a Hawaiian tradition of the lava dwellers that goes further. When the volcano erupts, and the lava rolls down the slopes to take away your home, Hawaiians say, "It is only Pele being Pele." There is no way to fight the goddess of fire; take what you can take, and then surrender your home. Some even say, "Don't just surrender it: make a gift to Pele!" The house is painted and decorated, in anticipation of its destruction by the lava in a few days. It is a final act of generosity.

Death and its fear visit us unannounced. But if we listen carefully, Death becomes our guide, who invites us to enter our fear in the same way we have entered our wounds in the unexplored room. If Death becomes our trusted guide, then we may learn to give with generosity when it is our time.

We have defied taboo to talk about mortality, because we have seen how taboos can help us find our identity. Like our other stories, our concept of death can also be rewritten with light. But perhaps we catch the most brilliant facet of light from Death's shadow, when we notice the meaning of what has already happened to us. It is work anyone can do, and we don't have to wait until the end to do it.

At the end of my mom's life, her dementia had ironically taken away the ability she loved the most: her wit. She was no longer able to offer the comedic, snappy comebacks she had been known for. Her language was gone. Also gone were her perfectionism, her critical view of herself, and her critical view of us. When I came downstairs to see her in the evenings, she could only remember my name. Her face lit up with joy. We laughed and hugged. At the end, the only thing left was love. Love was her heart knowledge.

In our final moments, our heart knowledge is all we have left. Heart knowledge was always our greatest possession, and it is what colored and defined how we lived.

Heart knowledge will also define how we will die.

Reflection

Create a quiet moment in a quiet place. Sit comfortably with your feet on the floor and your back straight, if you can. Breathe in deeply, and then breathe out deeply. Do this again until you notice your body beginning to relax.

As your body relaxes, allow yourself to process this chapter. Notice if any feelings have begun to arise. Did you notice any fear? Anxiety? Grief?

Did you remember a story of loss from your past? Allow the emotions to surface and release them.

If you were told you had only seven years left to live, would you make any changes in your life? Would the things that are important to you now still be important?

Could Death ever become your adviser? Could you ever become comfortable with your own death?

Have you ever sat with what you would like for the end of your life to look?

Sit quietly with gentleness and kindness for yourself.

Allow yourself to imagine your own final passage.

What does your heart "know" about this final process?

Were there any sounds or images that came to you?

What does your heart want to tell you?

Breathe in deeply, and then exhale fully. Open your eyes when you are ready to come back to the room where you are sitting.

Chapter Thirteen
Down the Stairs

Hey, daddy-o
I don't want to go down to the basement
There's somethin' down there

—THE RAMONES

Congratulations. You made it to chapter 13. No, there will not be a quiz. But there will be some homework. You are now invited to go down the stairs and enter your own unexplored room.

If you think about it carefully, you may notice that in this book, whenever my life changed for the better, it was not because of something I read. Transformation occurred because of something I experienced. Your heart can only learn from experience. Finishing this book is graduation, but your internship awaits you.

In Peter Jackson's movie *The Fellowship of the Ring*, Frodo and Sam walk across a farmer's field as they leave their home. Sam stops cold and says to Frodo, "This is it."

Frodo asks, "This is what?"

"If I take one more step, it will be the farthest away from home I've ever been."

Frodo smiles, comes back to Sam, and puts his arm around his shoulder. "Come on, Sam."

Sam takes a step forward. This is the beginning of an adventure neither of them can imagine.

Stepping down the stairs is just like that. You can do this. It is OK to feel a little resistance about going down those stairs. Everyone feels it—even the Ramones.

Anybody can do this work. I sit in a men's circle most weeks, and every time we meet, we all ask one another a question: "What is your work tonight?" Experience is always part of our work, and going into our unexplored rooms isn't a big deal to us anymore. It is how we live.

How to *start* your work is another question entirely. You might start by asking, "How do I find a good therapist?" It's not that hard. The best way to find someone is to follow your heart, because your heart is wise and intelligent. It knows more than you do.

There are a lot of choices out there. One classic choice comes from the movies. You can see psychiatrists, and in reality, they don't look much like Sigmund Freud any longer. Psychiatrists are physicians who are trained to prescribe medications and support mental illnesses like depression, addiction, or anxiety disorders, to name a few. If you want to talk in greater depth about your unexplored room, some psychiatrists might take the time to go there with you. But more often, they will partner with other professionals, such as psychologists, to do this. If you need to talk about your issues, the ones who don't do in-depth "talk therapy" typically know who the good therapists are. If you are struggling with depression, panic, or other symptoms and medication is necessary, then a psychiatrist is a great place to start.

Some therapists are psychologists, with PhDs in clinical psychology. These therapists have trained to do therapy and have had to do their own therapy as a part of their training. Other trained therapists may have advanced degrees in sociology or social work.

My first referral to such a therapist was made by my psychiatrist, who I was seeing as a part of my recovery program for drugs and alcohol. My psychiatrist could see clearly that I had issues to work on and referred me to a woman with a PhD in clinical psychology. I found her to be kind and sensitive, with powerful listening skills. Sometimes she would ask me one subtle question, and it would completely reframe how I was looking at my own life.

Many years later, I wanted to reenter therapy after becoming clean and sober through my work in a twelve-step fellowship. This time, I talked to my AA sponsor, who had also been in therapy himself. He recommended someone he had personally done work with. This psychologist proved to be another wonderful choice, and he helped me to look at how the relationships in my life were affecting me. If you have a trusted friend who has done his or her own personal work, he or she probably knows a therapist with a good reputation. Ask for help, and look for synchronicity; when you are ready, a therapist will appear.

Years later, I realized I wanted to work with someone who specialized in attachment disorders that may be seen in adopted kids. This time, I searched the Internet and found a psychology practice that specialized in attachment. I called and made an appointment. The woman I described in chapter 7 proved to be a kind, talented family therapist with an MSW degree. She deeply understood attachment, and I did some of my best work with her.

I think trustworthiness was a core quality that all my therapists held. They did not seem to have an agenda about how to fix me or about how I needed to change. All of them had been in therapy themselves, and all of them had worked on their own issues. They were human.

Often you can sense these qualities of authenticity and trustworthiness on the first visit in the therapist's office. It is partly about the therapist's vibe and also about the work he or she has done in order to sit with us. But it is equally important to notice the chemistry that forms between you and this person who will go with you into the unexplored room. Sometimes you might find a great therapist who may not be the right one for you. If you find one you can't work with, just write a check and say good-bye. Your heart will know.

Traditional talk therapy is a wonderful way to enter the unexplored room. I don't think it is possible to find a therapist who isn't familiar with the unexplored room, because this is a very old idea, and there are many other names for it. Therapy is the safest space where we can acknowledge our hidden material. For us to even admit to the existence of our concealed material with another human being is a courageous first step. Journaling is helpful, reflective, and solitary work, but therapy is different. Therapy is a trust piece in vulnerability.

In my first experience with therapy, I used to bring my journal along and read it to my therapist. I reached a personal milestone when I finally trusted her enough to just talk with her instead of reading my journal. I began to learn it could be safe to open my heart to another person.

Therapy is definitely a way to climb down the stairs to the unexplored room. Therapists are powerful witnesses to our work, and they affirm the truth of what we see about ourselves. It is also possible to be in therapy for a while and still feel stuck with the same old issues. If this happens, it is because we need more than a mindful analysis of our interior to reach a breakthrough. Classic talk therapy doesn't always reintegrate the emotions of the unexplored room like experience can. Experiential therapies open our hearts when we are ready.

Experiential work uses right-brained activities such as drama, music, dance, and art. It is the right side of the brain that holds the key to healing the unconscious parts of our psyche. Experience is at the center of my story. It was my experience of twelve-step work that first led me to understand I was enough. It was at an experiential retreat in the mountains of Pennsylvania that I first said hello to my core abandonment wounds. My experiences with my partner are what helped me to acknowledge my own triggers, and my home-made ceremonies helped me rewrite my life with new headlines. It was my experience of getting a tattoo that helped me make peace with my interior struggles. Countless workshops and weekly work with men's groups have helped me to own and understand my unexplored room. Experience is the core message of this book.

My first real breakthrough was in the week-long retreat described in chapter 4, where skilled therapists used techniques sometimes referred to as "psychodrama." Experiential programs like this allow clients to relive pivotal moments from their lives, as other clients stand in and even role-play as family members or people from their past. This kind of work is offered by many psychiatric and especially addiction-oriented treatment facilities. If you are working with a therapist, chances are high that your therapist may know of programs like this in your area.

Experienced facilitators create symbolic spaces, where clients can do powerful work. One leader in this field is Cliff Barry, who developed the Shadow Work® retreats and trainings offered around the world. Some of my personal work described in this book was in the context of this work and I am trained as a Shadow Work® facilitator. This form of facilitation is one way for us look at, integrate, and reframe our shadow material in a symbolic space. I have listed details of this and other resources at the end of the appendix.

Even though I write from a perspective of secular spirituality, it may be important to find experiential work within your own religious tradition. For example, when I was experimenting with the idea of what church membership might feel like for me, I learned about Christian-oriented work in the unexplored room. I saw a psychiatrist who used a technique called "Theophostic counseling" in his practice. Developed by a Baptist minister named Ed Smith, Theophostic prayer facilitates reimagining traumatic events within a symbolic framework of Christian prayer. In theophostic prayer, the client is asked to picture a traumatic event, and then is guided by the thera- pist to reimagine the event in the context of a prayer. Some have criticized this technique, but I found it to be helpful. Like all therapy, its effectiveness depends on the personal work of the facilitator.

Experiential retreats and workshops are available within many faith traditions. If you are in twelve-step recovery, there are fourth- and fifth-step retreats everywhere that invite this kind of work. I have personally worked with Rabbi Gershon Winkler, who offers Kabbalah workshops. There are Sufi workshops and Christian work- shops. If you are open to it, synchronicity will lead your heart to find your next workplace.

There are other experiential options for personal growth outside the rooms of traditional talk therapy. Over the years, I have had tremendous help from mentors, coaches, and intuitive counselors. One personal mentor and coach I have worked with over the years is a psychologist, futurist, and motivational speaker who has men- tored countless executives. He is the one who provided me with the "soul covenant" assignments to help me see the treasure con- cealed in my unexplored room. Skillful mentoring can help us ac- cess our own potential.

In a way, this book also provides a small taste of what mentoring could be like. Mentors are those who have already done this work. We then share how we did it, as I have done in the preceding chap- ters. Part of my professional work these days is to mentor physicians who want to learn a kind of laser treatment for lung cancer. This laser treatment was a part of my research work in the past, and the mentoring I do comes from my personal experience. Mentorship for personal growth involves a kind of sharing that arises from personal experience. Mentored sharing has a direct quality of disclosure that is usually not found in traditional talk therapy.

Similarly, personal coaches push us to reach our potential by challenging us. Coaches try to get us to perform at our edge. Intuitive counselors sense who we are, and then call to our attention unseen aspects of our unexplored room. They too provide us with assignments that change our lives. I have worked with intuitive counselor Sarah Entrup for many years, and it was Sarah who challenged me to start to do the men's work described in chapter 11.

When we are ready to work with a personal mentor, coach, or intuitive counselor, we will have to show up with a level of trust that is greater than what is needed for traditional therapy. This is because these mentored relationships offer us concrete suggestions about what we should do next. The trust we learn is a bridge that leads us to show up with vulnerability in the other relationships of our lives. Partitions between the sections of our lives come down, and we become the same person to everyone. We become trustworthy.

It is much easier to take suggestions from someone who speaks from his or her own experience. We also require a deeper level of trust if we enter an experiential program for personal work. It may seem a little scary to imagine working on our personal material in a group setting, but doing this is affirming in a powerful way. We see others doing the same work as we are. Affirmation enables us to become unstuck and move forward with our lives.

There may be some hazards if we venture down the stairs in this way. When I was early in recovery from drugs and alcohol, I had been in therapy before I considered the residential, week-long re-treat. I was told by those who ran the program that I needed to be clean and sober for at least nine months. After I went through this program, I could see why. Bringing out this kind of painful material, and re-experiencing it is precisely what can trigger relapse in clients who are in early recovery.

Doing work in our unexplored room can certainly bring up intense emotional pain, and this was the same pain I had medicated with drugs and alcohol. Once my recovery was stable, with a solid support system and a routine of self-care, I was then ready to descend the steps. When I returned home from my experiential work, I started at-tending new support-group meetings every week, in addition to my regular twelve-step meetings. If you are early in recovery, it is a great idea to get a solid foundation before trying deeper experiential work.

There is another danger. In many cases, the material stored away in our unexplored room is traumatic. It may be that sexual abuse or molestation is a part of our past. It may be that there was physical or emotional trauma, related to military service or other circumstanc-es. Those who have a history of post-traumatic stress disorder or PTSD often struggle with fragmented sleep, recurrent nightmares, and panic attacks. Flashbacks may be another feature of PTSD, and especially when doing drama-based work, there is a real possibility that vivid flashbacks might be triggered. If old trauma is triggered in this way, it can produce severe despair or even suicidal thoughts. Some experiential programs are not designed for those with PTSD.

For this reason, if we have a history of trauma, panic, recurring nightmares, or flashbacks, it is critical for us to share this informa-tion with the leaders of any program we consider entering. This is particularly true if it is a program that uses drama to recreate and rewrite old events from the past. Some of these techniques may be too intense for those of us with this condition.

But this does not mean help is unavailable for PTSD: There are many other ways to do healing work with traumatic material when it clings to the unexplored room. Across the country is a growing consciousness of PTSD, and "trauma programs" are designed specifically for those who have struggled with PTSD. These programs are created with safety in mind. I have personally witnessed the life-changing effect of such trauma work in those who are close to me.

There are also specialized programs designed for PTSD that resulted from military service. This kind of trauma may be emotional or physical and may stem from sexual abuse. I have been a board member for a program called "Warrior Heart to Art," which is a part of the nonprofit national group of retreats known as "Warrior Songs." These retreats were created for those who have PTSD from military service. They use the creative arts, along with music and community support, to explore the undiscovered room, and they create a powerful healing space among veterans. I have also witnessed remarkable personal work when I have attended such retreats.

Even if we have never been treated for PTSD, we still may have painful or dangerous material concealed in our unexplored room. If we stumble upon this frightening material when doing our work, there is a reliable part of us that warns us to stop.

Cliff Barry is one who teaches that such resistance comes from a trustworthy, internal sense of safety. This sense functions like a "protector," who has created space between us and the things that were scary, especially when we were small. If we face adult situations that seem threatening, this old part of us may keep us from working further.

If this kind of resistance occurs in the framework of Shadow Work®, the resistance is honored. While some programs are designed to push us to our edge in initiation, programs like Shadow Work® are based on a "consent model," where no process happens without our complete consent. Consent is a cornerstone of safety.

Gender is another important part of our work and concerns our sexual identity and how we express ourselves. Society has not been particularly generous on this point. When she was twenty-two, Miley Cyrus was quoted by *Out* magazine as saying, "I think that's what I had to understand: Being a girl isn't what I hate; it's the box that I get put into." Our culture has traditionally imposed masculine and feminine roles onto each of us. These roles determine what our life experience will be like. Any unacceptable aspect of gender expression is stowed away in the unexplored room.

For example, many women are taught that only certain behaviors are permitted when they are girls. They may leave childhood feeling it is shameful to be assertive or to defend themselves. When this is an expectation, achievement and boundaries are moved into the unexplored room.

There are a spectrum of identities between the poles of "male" and "female," because gender is more complicated than genetics: it is also determined by hormones, anatomy, psychology, and culture.

The emotional stress that LGBT individuals live with—and especially those with transgender issues—is responsible for higher rates of depression and suicide. Gender identity and sexual preference are a matter of heart knowledge. Understanding and owning our internal masculine and our internal feminine is part of everyone's work.

As men, uncovering and dealing with our roster of material can be easier with the nurturing and support of other men. And if we are women, there is also a kind of powerful synergy in the company of other women who are doing this work. If we decide to do gender-based retreats or groups, it is a good idea to seek advice from the group leader to make sure gender identity and sexual preferences are honored. It is important to find a safe work space.

I have had many conversations with Suzi about this, because she is keenly interested in women's spiritual work. She has found that women's work often focuses on helping women to trust and connect with their bodies. Such work may include dance and musical ritual within a symbolic space. My experience of men's work has been that drama is often used within a symbolic space. For feminine or masculine styles, this work can help us to learn about and honor our interior.

In some ways, I was one who grew up in the company of women, and I was always more comfortable being with women than with men. I wasn't any good at sports, and I never felt like I fit very well with traditional men's activities. I had many masculine issues hidden in my unexplored room. My intuitive counselor was the one who suggested I attend an experiential initiation for men, based on the shadow work of Robert Bly, the *Hero's Journey* work of Joseph

Greg Loewen

Campbell, and the archetypal work of Douglas Gillette and Robert Moore.

Imagine being in the company of a hundred men who have all worked on their shadows and who now have assembled as a team to help you work on yours. I can honestly say that learning to enjoy the companionship of men was only the first of many experiences that changed my life. A list of men's and women's retreats is found in the appendix that follows.

Finally, having a quiet, centering practice can be a remarkable addition to our quest to integrate our unseen interior. This usually means meditation in one of its many forms. But it is also possible to meditate a lot and to completely avoid personal work.
Meditation is not the same as working in the unexplored room, and unfortunately, many gurus have shown us this already. Meditation is not the same thing as inner work. It is like a flashlight we can take with us in order to help us see our work more clearly.

I think my own practice of meditation deepened my personal work. All kinds of emotions and thoughts naturally come up when we are triggered. Feelings are unavoidable if we look at loss, illness, or death. A practice of quiet stillness can give us neutrality and mindfulness, as described in chapter 10. It helps us to get outside of ourselves, because inside our stillness, we see we are not our feelings; instead, we are only conscious beings who experience feelings. We are able to get above ourselves and our emotions, and it is then safer for us to go deeper.

The work that awaits us down the stairway has been called our "descending" work. This contrasts with the "ascending" work of meditation and mindfulness. This is why I have ended every chapter with a reflection. It was my intention to offer a small taste of ascending work, as we examine the descending work of the unexplored room. Suzi teaches meditation to her clients as a part of her practice, and I am indebted to her for assisting me in writing the reflections at the ends of the preceding chapters.

Combining the ascending and descending aspects of personal work is a concept that is evolving. One pioneer in this area is Jun Po, formerly known as Dennis Kelly, who is responsible for creating a new Zen tradition in North America, known as Mondo Zen. He once told me it was his intention to combine the warrior Renzi tradition of personal work with a mindfulness practice, leaving behind any trace of religious doctrine.

In the Zen tradition, a Koan is a paradoxical question that is used to create doubt and to test the student. ("What is the sound of one hand clapping?" is a famous one.) There are over a thousand Koans in Zen, but Mondo Zen has picked thirteen specific Koans to help integrate our unconscious material. The Koan mentoring is done within the context of a mindfulness practice, and this is a powerful combination indeed. It was during a Zen retreat where I experienced my first satori that I experienced my personal power and my heart space as one. Many of the ideas found in this book came to me during Mondo Zen sessions.

Finally, in this book, I have played the part of physician, poet, and storyteller. I have merely described my own journey of experiential work with a picture like what I might use to describe a new treatment for one of my patients. Even though this map of the unexplored room makes sense for me, I would be the last to insist that my word picture is the only way to imagine our interior. But under-standing this has helped me look at myself with gentleness. If what you have read has helped you too, I am grateful. From my heart, I send you courage to do this work. You can do this.

Appendix

I promised this would be a book without references, because it was my intention to keep it from feeling like some kind of scientific research paper. On the other hand, you might like to know more about the songs, books, movies, and experiences that influenced me. Perhaps you would even like to explore them in your own personal work. So here you go. But first, a word about safety.

Safety Warning

Anytime we work in the unexplored room, it is possible to uncover things from the past that make us feel bad. Sometimes, really bad. So this part is about safety. When you are doing this work and a feeling of despair comes up, please talk to someone about what you are feeling. *Despair is only an emotion, but it is the worst secret that anyone can keep.* If you feel an impulse to do self-harm, or if suicidal thoughts come up, please tell someone. If you related with my story and have realized that you need help, tell your doctor. Open up with a friend. Be honest with another professional. Or if you prefer to talk on the phone to someone who doesn't know you, you can call the National Suicide Prevention Lifeline: 1-800-273-TALK (8255).

There is even a way to text for help: Crisis Text Line is open to people of all ages, and it provides free assistance to anyone who texts "help" to 741-741.

I encourage you with all my heart: help is available for you. This is the core message of this book.

The Soundtrack to the Unexplored Room

If this book were a movie, it would definitely have a soundtrack. So here it is, with my liner notes. Go ahead and make yourself a playlist, just for fun.

"Waters of March—Águas de Março" by Tom Jobim.
https://www.youtube.com/watch?v=wBEesrdaRog.
This is the YouTube video link to "Waters of March," or "Águas de Março," from chapter 1. In this performance in Portuguese, all the humor and joy that I love is captured by Elis Regina and Tom Jobim. Jobim is reported to have said that transcribing this kind of stream of consciousness was his version of therapy and saved him thousands in psychoanalysis bills. I also love the way Art Garfunkel covers this one in English.

"The Load-Out/Stay" by Jackson Browne from the album *Running on Empty* (1977).
Here is a YouTube video: https://www.youtube.com/watch?v=z3HecerzB0I. *Browne creates a great twist on the Four Season's*

original tune. This song from chapter 2 captures what it is like for me to love the connection with your audience as a performer.

"What's Broken" by David Crosby from the album *Croz* (2014). Another YouTube video https://www.youtube.com/watch?v= RZgBhyU4IvQ.
I have followed David Crosby since I was a kid, and I think his current work on this album is some of his best ever. For me, this song is deeply spiritual and seems to come from being enough to do the kind of work that this book is about.

"Digging in the Dirt" by Peter Gabriel from the album *Us* (1992). Here is a YouTube video released for this song: https://www. youtube.com/watch?v=X0C3DHp36zc.
Peter's video won the Grammy Award for Best Short Form Music Video in 1993 and explores self-healing that he was looking for in therapy. I especially love the imagery of getting dirt under my fingernails if I show up, willing to enter the wound.

"Little Lion Man" by Marcus Mumford from the album *Sigh No More* (2009). Here is a video from YouTube: https://www.youtube. com/watch?v=Xd8tOAJMA8Q.
Marcus Mumford commented that this song "represented the harder, darker side of what we do." To me, it is about our visitors from below.

"There's a Place in the World for a Gambler" by Dan Fogelberg from the *Souvenirs* album (1974). Another video from YouTube: https://www.youtube.com/watch?v=srNvp7w341I. *This song says to me that there's treasure in the darkest parts of the unexplored room.*

"All You Have to Do is Stay" by Taylor Swift from the album *1989* (2014). https://www.youtube.com/watch?v=OGG0JbrhGhM. *It took me a while to figure out it was that simple. What a great song.*

"The Rewrite" by Paul Simon from the album *So Beautiful, So What* (2011). Here's his live performance of the song: https://www.youtube.com/watch?v=yom8vZ7IEnQ.
In many ways, this is my favorite Simon album ever, and that's saying a lot. I always find his lyrics to be deeply spiritual, but this song really captures the ironic humor of reframing my life, as in chapter 8.

"That Don't Make It Junk" by Leonard Cohen from the album *Ten New Songs* (2001). Here is a YouTube of his song: https://www.youtube.com/watch?v=DYmF8AIqR4E.
I love Leonard's poetry, and I think that he knew a lot about feelings. May he rest in peace. His line about how transient feelings are is probably the most important part of chapter 9.

"In the Blood" off John Mayer's album *The Search for Everything* (2017). Here is the YouTube for this amazing song: https://www.youtube.com/watch?v=ob-jS7bqYgI.
John's song made me cry the first time I heard it. I have lived this song.

"I Saw the Sign" by Jonas Bergen from the album *Happy Nation* by Ace of Base (1992). https://www.youtube.com/watch?v=UElAPvz6Hel. *I recognize that this song probably isn't about the Jungian concept of synchronicity in chapter 11, but it could be, with a little projection.*

"Lazarus" by David Bowie from the album *Blackstar* (2016). You really need the visual to fully appreciate his work on this one: https://

www.youtube.com/watch?v=y-JqH1M4Ya8. *I laughed when I first saw Bowie's video, where he plays with death, right in front of everyone.*

"I Don't Wanna Go Down to the Basement" by the Ramones from *Ramones* (1976).
https://www.youtube.com/watch?v=maS68s9jpYo. *Ramones. They seemed to articulate this feeling the best. Enough said.*

A bonus track for the end of the album.
"What Am I Supposed to Do?" by Hicks, Nikki, and the Soul Music Souljahs. This live performance at the University of Buffalo Center for the Arts was recorded in 2010 on YouTube. https://www.youtube.com/watch?v=EUnuJhM7yXA. *The soulful Nikki Hicks. We wrote this song together. I played with Nikki for years in the club scene in Buffalo.*

Bookshelf

Here are a few books and articles that I brought upstairs from my unexplored room, as a possible reading list for you. The more time you spend working down there, the more new books will show up on your own bookshelf.

Anonymous. *Alcoholics Anonymous: The Big Book.* New York: Alcoholics Anonymous World Services, 1939. *You don't have to be an alcoholic to appreciate the spiritual wisdom found here. I have read it many times.*

Aristotle. *Neomachean Ethics,* Athens, Greece, 350 BC. *Aristotle's ideas are still relevant nearly twenty-four hundred years later. My wife brought this book home as a part of the reading list for a spirituality course that she took.*

Bly, Robert. *Little Book on the Human Shadow.* New York: HarperCollins, 1988. *This tiny book is very profound, and I was excited when I found out that it was required reading for a men's workshop that I attended. It is truly a spiritual classic.*

Bly Robert, and Hillman, James. *Men and the Wild Child*. Boulder, CO: Sounds True, 1990. *This is an audiobook live recording of Robert Bly at a men's retreat, this time with James Hillman, who talks about the bullfighter in chapter 8.*

Bradshaw, John. *Homecoming*. New York: Bantam Books, 1990. *I found that this book really helped me, early in my recovery. John's audiobook exercises of the same title (which included the music of Steven Halpern) helped me to zero in on where my greatest injuries were hidden.*

Byock, Ira. *Dying Well: Peace and Possibilities at the End of Life*. New York: Riverhead Books, 1997. *Ira's work really changed the way I practice medicine, especially for patients who are facing the end of life.*

Campbell, Joseph. *The Hero with a Thousand Faces*. Novato, CA: New World Library, 1949. *Campbell helped me recognize how we all resonate with this universal story.*

Capra, Fritjof. *The Tao of Physics*. Boulder CO: Shambhala Press, 1975.
Fritjof's book is really more about Tao than physics, and some of the ideas in chapter 11 originated here.

Chopra, Deepak, Debbie Ford, and Marianne Williamson. *The Shadow Effect*. New York: Harper One, 2010. *In his section, I thought that Deepak nailed it when he suggested that the way to combat the influence of the shadow is by achieving wholeness. In the second portion of the book, the late Debbie Ford tells her own stories to show how the things that we hate may come to visit us. I really related to this. In the final section, I resonated when Marianne suggests that we can only escape the darkness of our shadow by outgrowing it.*

Clarke, David. *They Can't Find Anything Wrong: 7 Keys to Understanding, Treating, and Healing Stress Illness.* Boulder, CO: First Sentient Publications, 2007. *Clarke discusses what he has learned about stress-related illness from his patients. I heard him speak once in Spokane, and I totally related to his experiences with patients who develop physical symptoms from their stress.*

Dass, Ram. *Be Here Now.* New York: Three Rivers Press, 1971. *On the outside, it looks like a graphic novel from the sixties, but on the inside, it is filled with wisdom. A spiritual classic.*

Deida, David. *The Way of the Superior Man: A Spiritual Guide to Mastering the Challenges of Women, Work, and Sexual Desire.* Boulder, CO: Sounds True, 2004.
I found David's writing challenging at first, and I was forced to relook at my own masculinity. He helped me to show up in a new way. I have gone back to this book many times, and I have also consistently recommended it to men I have mentored.

Ebert, Roger. *Life Itself.* New York: Grand Central Publishing, 2011. *Roger's book (and the movie about Roger by the same name) inspires me to say that I think he might be one of the bravest men I have ever witnessed. May he rest in peace, and I don't care if he disagrees with me.*

Drummond, Dike. *Stop Physician Burnout.* Collinsville, MS, Heritage Press Publications, 2014. *Dike is a Mayo family physician who started*

"The Happy MD" to address the epidemic of physician burnout. His best seller is a workbook that focuses on practical ways to make self-care part of your life. I liked what Dike is doing, but I also had a feeling that there is a deeper injury that some of us physicians live with, if we are on the front lines of death and trauma every day.

Foos Graber, Anya. *Deathing: An Intelligent Alternative for the Final Moments of Life.* Lake Worth, FL: Nicholas Hays, 1989. *Anya's creative book is part novel and part essay, but it gave me a new way of thinking about the dying process.*

Ford, Deborah. *The Dark Side of the Light Chasers.* London, UK: Penguin Publishing Group, 1998. *I loved Debbie's book, which focuses primarily on how we can learn about our shadow if we pay attention to the images and judgments that we project on others.*

Frankl, Victor. *Man's Search for Meaning.* Boston: Beacon Press, 1946. *I have read his courageous story many times, and it inspires me each time I go there.*

Gottman, John. *The Seven Principles for Making Marriage Work: A Practical Guide from the Country's Foremost Relationship Expert.* New York: Three Rivers Press, 1999. *I have referred to John's pivotal work on relationships in chapter 7.*

Gundersen, Linda. "Physician Burnout." *Annals of Internal Medicine* 135 (2) (2001): 145–48. *I thought that Gundersen's discussion of physician burnout zeroes in on the idea of self-care, which is so important. One thing that is underappreciated in physician burnout is the potential of PTSD, especially in specialties like mine (pulmonary critical care) and emergency medicine. The trauma that caregivers witness and participate in is not completely like a war zone.*

Hendrix, Harville. *Getting the Love You Want*. New York: Macmillan Publishers, 2007. *Hendrix outlines a kind of couple's therapy that is another form of shadow work for relationships, called "Imago Therapy."*

Herman, Judith Lewis. *Trauma and Recovery*. New York, NY, Basic Books, 1992. *Dr. Herman's groundbreaking work draws parallels between trauma from sexual abuse and trauma from PTSD from combat as seen in veterans. She also explores the fabric of understanding that General Patton lived in and how and why this has evolved over time.*

Hyemeyohsts Storm. *Seven Arrows*. New York, NY, Harper & Row, 1972. *I learned about this book from Klara Adalena, who is mentioned below. I found this collection of traditional Native American stories to be remarkable and profound.*

Jung, Carl G. *The Portable Jung*. Edited by Joseph Campbell, translated by R. F. C. Hull. City of Westminster, London, UK: Penguin Books, 1971. *Carl Jung is credited with the concept of the human shadow, which I have reimagined in this book. It seemed to me that an unexplored room full of stuff might free us from the judgment that our shadow is some kind of internal "darkness" that we carry around.*

Love, Patricia. *The Emotional Incest Syndrome: What to Do When a Parent's Love Rules Your Life*. New York: Bantam Books, 1991.

Greg Loewen

Patricia Love's work really helped me to come to terms with what had made me so angry me for so long.

Marlantes, Karl. *What It Is Like to Go to War.* New York: Atlantic Monthly Press, 2011. *I can't adequately express how much I admire this brilliant and honest book, which describes the psychological injuries of war and also describes what work in the unexplored room might look like for a soldier who has served in active duty. His work makes me want to cheer.*

Martin-Smith, Keith. *A Heart Blown Open.* Studio City, CA, Divine Arts Media, 2012.
I loved Jun Po's authentic story of personal work and enlightenment, which I read after attending one of his Mondo Zen retreats.

Moore, Robert, and Doug Gillette. *King, Warrior, Magician, Lover: Rediscovering the Archetypes of the Mature Masculine.* New York: HarperCollins, 1990. *This classic book on men's archetypes is one that I recommend for the men whom I coach, and it has helped me to understand my own interior.*

Paulus, Trina. *Hope for the Flowers.* New York: Paulist Fathers Press, 1972.
It took me thirty years to get around to reading this book that Suzi gave me, and I was done with it in thirty minutes. And here I am, still talking about it.

Proulx, Annie. *The Shipping News.* New York: Scribner, 1993.
This is one of my favorite novels ever. It is a masterpiece that describes what it looks like to find your voice and change your headlines.

Robbins, Tom. *Still Life with Woodpecker*. New York: Bantam Books,1980. *In his satirical novel, Robbins asks the question that all victims (including me) have asked: "What is it that makes love stay?"*

Shinoda Bolen, Jean. *Close to the Bone*. Newburyport, MA: Conari Press, 1983. *I met Jean at a wisdom retreat in Colorado and loved her energy. In this book, she talks about how our shadow plays out in illness. Jean also has many other titles that are especially relevant for women's work with archetypes.*

Soll, Joe. *Adoption Healing*. Baltimore, MD: Gateway Press, 2000. *Joe's workbook focuses on issues that I have had as an adoptee, and for me, it was a trail of tears. Even though it was accessible and profound for me, not everyone will relate to it.*

Vissell, Barry and Vissell, Joyce. *The Shared Heart*. Aptos, CA: Ramira Publishing, 1984. *Barry and Joyce's insightful book about relationships really helped us, and so did working with them in person on their couple's retreat.*

Wilber, Ken. *Kosmic Consciousness*. Boulder, CO: Sounds True Incorporated, 2003.
Ken's audiobook holds nearly thirteen hours of interview with Tami Simon, which I found to be funny and brilliant. I have listened to it many times. The ideas of Truth, Goodness, and Beauty in chapter 1 might have come from the Greeks, but Ken made sense of it for me.

Zweig, Connie and Steve Wolf. *Romancing the Shadow: A Guide to Soul Work for a Vital Authentic Life*. New York: Ballantine Books, 1997. *Connie and Steve share their own stories in this book and explain the concepts of shadow with traditional Greek mythology*

Greg Loewen

in the Jungian fashion (which I have to admit that I struggle with). What I liked most was the breathing exercise that they describe and how to experience healing.

Blockbusters from the Shadow

Here are a few movies and videos mentioned in my narrative. They are rich in archetypes, and all were found in my unexplored room. I am sure that you will find your own collection of DVDs waiting for you, too, when you start exploring.

AI Artificial Intelligence (2001). Here is the IMDB link:
http://www.imdb.com/title/tt0212720/?ref_=nv_sr_1.
This film project was initially developed by the late Stanley Kubrick and thankfully was completed and directed by Steven Spielberg. I couldn't help but be drawn in by the powerful theme of abandonment.

Thanks for Sharing (2012). Here is the IMDB link:
http://www.imdb.com/title/tt1932718/?ref_=nv_sr_2.
This film is about sexual addiction and recovery, and I found it to be funny, sad, and true.

Brown, Brené (2012). "Listening to shame." Here is a link to Brené's famous TED talk:
https://www.ted.com/talks/brene_brown_on_vulnerability.

Brené Brown's viral talk on vulnerability was a big part of my inspiration for creating this book. If you haven't seen it, take a few minutes and watch this. Amazing.

Patch Adams (1998). Here is the IMDB page about the movie: http://www.imdb.com/title/tt0129290/.
The 1998 movie Patch Adams *starred the late comedic genius Robin Williams. I related to how the patients responded to humor when they were sick, and I liked how he played with a way of humanizing scientific medical care.*

Sunshine Cleaning (2008). Here is the IMDB page about the movie: http://www.imdb.com/title/tt0862846/?ref_=nv_sr_1.
This is one of my favorite movies and is classic viewing for any kind of bastard. The scene described in chapter 3 made me laugh and cry, the first time I saw it.

Patton (1971). Here is the IMDB page about the movie: http://www.imdb.com/title/tt0066206.
I talked about the hospital scene from this movie in chapter 5. The movie does not have adequate time to describe what military culture was like in that era, but in real life, General Patton was certainly not alone in his prejudices about soldiers with PTSD.

The Secret Life of Walter Mitty (2013). Here is the IMDB page about the movie:
http://www.imdb.com/title/tt0359950/?ref_=nv_sr_3.
This movie is directed by (and starring) Ben Stiller. It takes James Thurber's original story and goes much deeper with it. I loved how the Ben Stiller character was able to find what he loved as a kid. It

is an example of the treasure that can be found in the unexplored room.

To Kill a Mockingbird (1962). Here is the IMDB page about the movie:
http://www.imdb.com/title/tt0056592/?ref_=nv_sr_1.
This is where I first learned about Atticus Finch and realized that I wanted to be like him.

Pollyanna (1960). Here is the IMDB page about the movie: http://www.imdb.com/title/tt0054195/. *This is where I learned about Pollyanna and realized that I wanted to be like her.*

The Mission (1984). Here is the IMDB site about the movie: http://www.imdb.com/title/tt0091530/. *For me, the image of Mendoza climbing the cliff as he drags the weight of his past life behind him in chapter 8 was unforgettable.*

Star Wars: Episode VI—Return of the Jedi (1983). Here is the IMDB site for the movie:
http://www.imdb.com/title/tt0086190/?ref_=nv_sr_1.
This is the Star Wars episode that contains the scene described in chapter 6, where Darth Vader removes his helmet and connects with his son, at the end of his life.

Inside Out (2015). Here is the IMDB link: http://www.imdb.com/title/tt2096673/?ref_=nv_sr_1. *I have watched this insightful 3-D computer-animated film about emotions several times. I think that what I love the most is how a maligned and dreaded emotion (like sadness) completely saves the day. For me, this is the power of grief work.*

The Natural (1984). Here is the IMDB link: http://www.imdb.com/ title/tt0087781/. *The scene at the end of the movie described in chapter 12, when Roy hits a home run, symbolized the end of life for me.*

Living in the Material World (2011). Here is the IMDB link: http:// www.imdb.com/title/tt1113829/. *This warm, insightful documentary directed by Martin Scorsese stars George Harrison, Paul McCartney, John Lennon, Ringo Starr, Olivia Harrison, and many others. I found the account of the end of George's life both touching and inspiring.*

Road trips

Finally, here are some road trips from chapter 13. Even though they start on your computer screen, many of them will beckon you to leave the house on an adventure. Listen to your heart on this one. It knows more than you do.

https://warriorsongs.org/home.
This link leads to information about the Warrior Song retreats, which I mentioned again in chapter 13. Suzi and I support their organization and attend their community performances when we are able to.

https://projectsemicolon.com/.
I belong to this project, which was created by Amy Bleuel, who was lost to suicide in 2017.

http://qprinstitute.com/.
This is a link to QPR training: Question, Persuade, Refer. It is a suicide-intervention training that is available for health-care professionals and laypersons, too. It is like CPR for suicide. Brilliant. Easy.

It takes a few hours online, and if you learn it, you might save some-one's life.

https://therapists.psychologytoday.com/rms/.
This is a web tool from Psychology Today that can help find a psy-chologist or therapist in your area.

https://www.caron.org/.
This is the Caron Foundation website: they are a nonprofit organiza-tion of treatment resources that focus on addiction and offer expe-riential therapy, as described in this book.

http://www.shadowwork.com/.
Shadow Work® seminars created by Cliff Barry and others offer ex-periential personal work in the settings of either group or individual counseling. They also offer training and certification for facilitation skills.

http://www.theophostic.com/.
Here is a link to the Theophostic prayer resources mentioned in chapter 13.

The Ford Institute was founded by author Debbie Ford.
http://www.thefordinstitute.com. *Here is a link to the Ford Institute for Transformational Training. The Ford Institute offers both one-on-one coaching and an experiential workshop called "The Shadow Experience."*

http://www.kaiser.net/.
Here is a link to the Kaiser Institute, which offers experiential devel-opment sessions and one-on-one coaching for executive leadership.

I once had the opportunity to attend their Intuition Program years ago, and I found it to be life-changing.

http://sarahentrup.com/wp/. *Here is a link to the website for Sarah Entrup, who holds a master's degree in divinity. Sarah offers insightful and creative guided meditations, intuitive readings, and coaching and is an international leader in women's work.*

https://www.ptsd.va.gov/public/treatment/therapy-med/treatment-ptsd.asp.
Here is a link to further information on PTSD, offered by the US Department of Veterans Affairs.

https://warriorsongs.org/home.
Here is a link to the Warrior Song programs. They are not affiliated with the US Department of Veterans Affairs. I also mentioned this resource in chapter 5.

http://mankindproject.org/. *I cannot say enough about how much the Mankind Project and other men's work programs have helped me. If your heart resonates with my description of men's work, please check this out. There are many open groups that meet in the evening for an hour or two, and there is probably one where you live.*

http://www.innerking.com/. *More advanced men's work that also really helped me. Highly recommended.*

http://www.klaraadalena.com/.
Klara Adalena's work with women draws from Joseph Campbell's idea of the hero's journey. They use a powerful nonverbal approach

Greg Loewen

to work in the unexplored room with transformational ritual and sacred dance.

http://www.mondozen.org/.
Finally, here is a link to the Mondo Zen tradition, which—in its own words—"transcends the hierarchical/authoritarian, gender-biased, and constraining monastic aspects of traditional Zen in favor of practical, experiential 'in the world' engagement." The empty interval found within Mondo sessions was remarkably helpful to me as I prepared this book.

There are countless experiential programs for shadow work, trauma work, men and women's work, and meditation that I have not included. This is primarily because I have limited my list to things I have either personally experienced or experienced indirectly through others. My appendix is in no way meant to exclude all the other good work that is out there. If you have experience with other programs that were helpful with your work in the unexplored room, I would love to hear from you.

Made in the USA
San Bernardino, CA
21 June 2017